REMEMBERING
POTTSTOWN

········ REMEMBERING ········

POTTSTOWN

HISTORIC TALES FROM A PENNSYLVANIA BOROUGH

Michael T. Snyder

THE
History
PRESS

Published by The History Press
Charleston, SC 29403
www.historypress.net

Front cover: (top) *Pottstown Historical Society*; (bottom) *Krause Collection.*
Back cover: (top) *Pottstown Historical Society*; (middle) *Library of Congress*; (bottom) *Pottstown Historical Society.*

First published 2010

Manufactured in the United States

ISBN 978.1.59629.842.2

Library of Congress CIP data applied for.

CONTENTS

CONTENTS

PREFACE

Pottstown is a fascinating community whose roots reach back more than 250 years. During that time, more than ten generations of Americans have lived here. The people of these generations were of the same stock as those of today. The vast majority wanted happiness and security and were willing to work hard to achieve those goals.

This book presents the lives of a few of the people who lived here during Pottstown's existence. It describes their daily life, their successes and their failures and links them to important events in American history.

ACKNOWLEDGEMENTS

Putting a book together is a complex process that requires contributions from many people besides the author. In the case of this work, John Strickler, a gifted photographer, cheerfully created the images that enhance it.

Mrs. Patricia Sommers, my editor at the *Pottstown Mercury*, has used her considerable skills in editing and proofreading to make improvements to the manuscript.

David Kerns, the Pottstown Historical Society's historian and the expert on the history of Pottstown, has generously shared his material. Other local historians who have contributed are Michael Osiol, Milton Yohn, Robert Wood, Estelle Cremers and Jack Ertell of the Phoenixville Historical Society.

Librarians and archivists who helped include Clara Hoss, librarian of the Pottstown Historical Society and a staff librarian at the Pottstown Public Library, who played a key role in locating materials in the collections of both institutions; Lou Jeffries of the Hill School Library; Gabriel Schecter of the Baseball Hall of Fame Library; Arlene Balkansky of the Library of Congress; and Lionel Green and his staff at the Montgomery County Records Archives.

The many people who gave interviews include: for World War II, Willard and Margaret (Robenolt) Bickel, Edward and Ann Jane (Case) Dobry, Gabe Fieni and Mrs. Mary Finn; for other subjects, Mrs. Jennie Beck, Richard Grey, Bill Krause, Robert Lamb, Dr. Carol Nathanson, Arlen Saylor and James Sheppard.

Acknowledgements

Also, many thanks to Bill Krause and George Wausnock for permission to photograph items from their collections.

I am also grateful to Hannah Cassilly, my editor at The History Press, who helped me shape this book and deftly guided me through the production process.

Finally, and most importantly, a special thanks to my wife, Mary Alice, who has encouraged me in everything I have done for the last forty-three years.

Part I

POTTSTOWN IN THE EIGHTEENTH CENTURY

A Tiny Village and a Nation Are Born

———•———

POTTSTOWN'S BEGINNINGS

The story of Pottstown's origins is inextricably bound to the development of the iron industry in colonial Pennsylvania. From the colony's early days, it was known that the land along Manatawny Creek just a few miles upstream from present-day Pottstown was rich in iron ore. In 1715, Thomas Rutter, a blacksmith from Germantown, bought three hundred acres of this land, and by 1716, he and his son-in-law had built the first ironworks in Pennsylvania on the property.

Rutter subsequently formed an investment company and built an iron furnace at Colebrook Dale, also the first of its kind in Penn's land. His success attracted an investor, Thomas Potts, a forty-five-year-old victualer from Germantown, who rented the properties in 1725. Initially, he tended to the financial end of the business, but he soon learned the trade's technical aspects and gradually purchased shares of Rutter's iron company, bought more land and built more forges in the area.

For more than a quarter of a century, Potts continued to improve and expand his iron business. By the time he died on January 4, 1752, his

Pottsgrove Manor, John Potts's home as it appears today. *Courtesy of John Strickler.*

development and implementation of mass production techniques had taken colonial iron manufacturing from a cottage industry and put it on the road to modern industrialization.

Shortly before Thomas Potts died, his oldest son, John (born in Philadelphia, 1709/10), took control of the firm's iron-making aspects. The fact that John's younger brother, Thomas, would inherit the family home at Colebrook Dale Furnace led to the birth of Pottstown. John Potts needed a new home, so in 1751 he bought 995 acres of land around the confluence of Manatawny Creek and the Schuylkill River from Samuel McCall.

There he had a forge built and running by July 7, 1752, and by the fall of 1753, he had moved his family into their new home, Pottsgrove, which still stands between High and King Streets just west of Manatawny Creek. The house was built on a hill, where it overlooked the Great Road that connected Philadelphia with Reading and allowed an unobstructed view of the Schuylkill River. Designed in the early Georgian style that was popular with the English gentry of that time, its massive walls, two feet thick, were made from sandstone quarried at nearby Glasgow Forge. Every aspect of its construction, both exterior and interior, was a tribute to Potts's success and symbolized the wealth and power that he had attained in colonial Pennsylvania.

When Potts moved to the McCall tract, he already had neighbors—a few cabins and a gristmill—and because of the construction of the forge, a few more houses would have been added for his employees. Potts eventually realized that by creating a town out of part of this land, he would have an income from lot sales and rents that was independent of the money he earned in the iron business. On November 25, 1761, a surveyor laid out the town, and Pottstown came into existence.

Potts was quick to market his new venture. Just a little over three weeks after the survey, an advertisement ran in the December 17, 1761 issue of the *Pennsylvania Gazette* (a Philadelphia newspaper) informing potential buyers that this new town, "to be called Pottsgrove," was in a great location for promoting "trade and commerce." It was "situated on the river Schuylkill" and had a good road network: the Great Road, which connected Philadelphia with Reading, and a road that ran north leading to Bethlehem and Easton and on to north New Jersey. The town's main street (present-day High Street), which followed the Great Road for part of its course, would be one hundred feet wide, while the road that ran north (present-day Hanover Street) would be eighty feet in width. The streets were laid out in a grid, and many of their names showed that the citizens of Pottsgrove were British subjects: Hanover because England's king was of that house, and York because his son, Frederick, was the Duke of York.

The town, which was very small, went from the Manatawny Creek east to Evans Street and, in the section east of Hanover, ranged from the Schuylkill River north to Chestnut Street, while west of Hanover its north–south range was only from High Street to Chestnut, or about 150 acres. Initially, there were sixty-eight double lots, each sixty by six hundred feet and fronting on High Street. In 1762, its area was expanded two blocks to the north with the addition of Walnut and Beech Streets, but it seems that lots in this addition were only three hundred feet deep.

As an additional incentive, Potts pledged "to give and make over unto any Twenty Families of the two first Denominations of Christians, that shall settle in the said Town, a convenient Lot for building a Place of Worship and School house, and half an Acre of Ground for a Burying Place." To that end, Potts donated to the Society of Friends half of a lot between Hanover and Penn Streets, where it erected Pottstown's first church—a small brick building on the north side of King Street, now a parking lot next to the Bell Telephone building. Continuing in the same vein, he offered a lot on the east side of Hanover between Chestnut and Walnut Streets to the Germans for a church and cemetery. In 1770, they took advantage of the offer and built a log church on the southeast corner of Chestnut and Hanover Streets.

Despite Potts's efforts, his new village didn't grow very fast. The Pottstown Forge ledger shows that in 1762, its first year, twenty-four of the sixty-eight lots were rented, and a study of early residents and land transfers during 1770 shows that twenty-seven lots were spoken for. Of these, probably only sixteen had houses on them.

The following is a description of a house in Pottstown that was for sale in 1764:

> *A complete two Story Stone House…29 Feet front, 36 deep, a Cellar under the whole, 30 Feet, Kitchen and Piazza two Story, 20 Feet, Stone Wash house, a 50 Feet Stable, two Story, all covered with Cedar, a large Garden, pailed* [fenced] *in the best Manner; a Well of good Water at the Kitchen door.*

By mid-eighteenth-century standards, this was a very attractive home, but there was only a little over two thousand square feet inside, which was pretty cramped compared to today's houses. Of course, there was no plumbing—water came from a hand-dug well that wasn't very deep—so depending on the location of the privy and other factors, the water may have been contaminated. The house was cold in the winter. In the summer it was hot, and there were no window screens, so if you opened the windows, you were beset by flies and mosquitoes that swarmed in from everywhere.

This glacial rate of expansion continued for the rest of the eighteenth century so that by 1800, Pottstown was still a sleepy little rural village with probably no more than four hundred inhabitants. Of course, some of John Potts's children and their families lived there, but for the most part its citizens were artisans, such as millers, coopers and tanners, or laborers and teamsters, along with a merchant or two and two or three innkeepers.

To further emphasize the village's rustic flavor, after thirty-nine years of existence, Pottstown was still not incorporated; its citizens were either residents of New Hanover or Douglas Township, and as a result, there was no burgess, no town council, no police and the carpenter doubled as the undertaker.

John Potts and his wife, Ruth Rutter, had thirteen children, who all lived to maturity. In the mid-eighteenth century, when children's deaths were a tragic fact of life, this is an amazing statistic. John Potts died on June 6, 1768, "after a long and tedious illness," at his house in Pottsgrove.

Ruth (Savage) Potts, wife of John
Potts. *Courtesy of Pottsgrove Manor.*

His obituary in the *Pennsylvania Gazette* referred to him as "a Gentleman
of unblemished Honour and Integrity." He is buried at the Potts Burial
Ground, in a small plot that sits unobtrusively on the south side of
Chestnut Street, just west of Penn, protected by a stone wall and a double
iron gate.

Ruth Potts outlived her husband by eighteen years, dying at Pottsgrove
on Saturday, January 7, 1786. She is buried next to him at the Potts Burial
Ground. An obituary in a Philadelphia paper, the *Pennsylvania Journal and
Weekly Advertiser*, stated, "She departed this life, aged seventy years, after
a short but severe illness, which she sustained with true resignation."

John Potts was wealthy and influential. He owned large parcels of
land and iron forges, farms and mills of all kinds in many counties in
Pennsylvania and Virginia. He owned several homes in Philadelphia,
along with stores, wharves and Pottsgrove, his 550-acre plantation and
showpiece mansion.

Potts historian Daniel Graham considers him to have been "the most
important iron manufacturer in Pennsylvania," noting that "he expanded
and enhanced his father's multi-forge production methods using his sons to

manage his various works and produced iron and iron products on a scale not seen elsewhere in the colonies." Graham also notes that Potts's influence did not end with his death because he left "a number of sons and grandsons to carry on the iron business…As a result, the Potts family remained in the Pennsylvania iron industry for generations."

POTTSTOWN DURING THE REVOLUTIONARY WAR

"A Pretty Town Whose People Are Tories"

On April 19, 1775, Massachusetts militiamen attacked British soldiers at Lexington and Concord. This battle set in motion a chain of events that led to the colonies declaring their desire to be free from Great Britain. This declaration resulted in a war for independence that lasted until 1781.

The population of Pottstown was so small during the war years that there were few men of military age living there, and because it was not incorporated, it had no tax lists, making it next to impossible to identify men who lived in Pottstown and served in the military during the war. However, because of contemporary testimony, it is known that some did. For instance, on August 16, 1776, Lutheran minister Reverend Henry Muhlenberg wrote in his journal:

> *Colonel Bird, Esq's battalion marched through here* [Trappe], *they were cheerful young men and riflemen, among whom are many of our members from New Hanover and Pottsgrove who waved an affectionate farewell as they went by like sheep and rams to the slaughter.*

In addition to these anonymous but "cheerful young men from Pottsgrove," there is a plaque on the lawn next to Zion's United Church of Christ that contains the names of people who were buried in the old church graveyard. Two men listed there—Christian Lessig (1745–1827) and George Bechtel (1744–1818)—are credited with military service, but it does not specify what kind.

And there is Jacob Drinkhouse from Pottstown, who witnessed the execution of the British spy Major John Andre at West Point, New York, on October 2, 1780, while serving with the army there. The legend continues that Drinkhouse climbed a tree to get a better view of the proceedings. He took off his shoes to make climbing easier. When he got back down, the shoes were gone, and he had to walk barefoot back to Pottstown.

Jacob Drinkhouse lived in a log house on High Street where he also conducted his harness- and saddle-making business. Drinkhouse, who was also the town's postmaster and a member of the Pennsylvania House of Representatives, died in 1858 at the age of ninety-seven; he was Pottstown's last surviving veteran of the War for Independence. Years later, a Pottstown resident remembered him as "tall and spare in stature, naturally sedate and dignified in his demeanor…and an honest and kind hearted man."

In September 1777, the war came right up to Pottstown's doorstep as the British entered southeastern Pennsylvania with the intention of capturing Philadelphia, the rebellion's capital and largest city. Supporters of the rebellion had no illusions about their fate if their cause failed—prison and confiscation of property for sure; hanging, very likely—and this knowledge made members of the Continental Congress and other leaders in Philadelphia very nervous and suspicious of possible traitors.

A group of Quakers identified by Congress as "disaffected to the American cause" was rounded up on September 4. On September 11, some of them were loaded into wagons and began a journey into exile in Winchester, Virginia. Their route took them on the Great Road and into Pottstown on the evening of the next day. News of their coming preceded them, and when their caravan pulled up at the Red Lion Inn, which was located on the south side of High Street on the east bank of Manatawny Creek, members of the Potts family, who probably knew most of the men, were there to greet them. "We reached this place at 8 o'clock last evening & were…kindly rec'd By the Senr Branches of the Pott's & have been courteously entertained."

Because the wagons carrying the prisoners' baggage had not arrived, they were permitted to stay another night. According to a September 15 entry in a Lancaster man's diary, the rumor mills of the time turned that extra time in Pottstown into something more sinister:

News of the day is that the Friends sent out of town as prisoners were stopped at Pottsgrove by the Pottes [sic] there, and they would not suffer them to proceed any further, upon which a company of militia was ordered from Reading to take them in charge and convey them to their destined post.

A company of twenty armed men was sent from Reading with orders to move them along, but there is no record of the Pottses or anyone else interfering. The exiles finally left Pottstown on the fourteenth, heading toward Reading and continuing their long trek to Virginia. They would not see their homes again until April 1778.

It is noteworthy that the Potts family, with the exception of John Jr., supported the American Revolution, and as far as is known, so did the rest of the people in the area. However, on July 17 an officer in the Continental army who passed through town wrote about coming to "Pottsgrove, a pretty town whose people are Tories. I put them to silence, but being informed that an insurrection might take place, I thought it advisable to cross the Schuylkill." At least one other man shared this opinion. On September 22, Samuel Chase, writing from Pottstown to George Washington concerning supplies stored in Pottstown, also thought that "in this place the Inhabitants are almost all Tories."

For William Dewees, a former Pottstown resident, the British occupation of southeastern Pennsylvania was a disaster. Dewees, born in 1723, married Sarah Potts, whose father was a half brother of John Potts, the founder of Pottstown. No doubt because of this strong Potts family connection, by 1763 William and his brother, Thomas, were living in Pottstown, where both kept taverns. Thomas Dewees was the proprietor of the Red Lion Inn on the south side of High Street, just east of Manatawny Creek, while William Dewees, who owned four lots in town, had a tavern located somewhere on the north side of High Street on a lot that extended 180 feet west from York.

In 1773, Dewees, in partnership with David Potts (another son of John Potts), bought Valley Forge. By September 1777, the operation had become a valuable industrial/residential complex that provided employment for millers and ironworkers and was home to two families. Unfortunately, its future was now in jeopardy.

In the early spring of 1777, American authorities, concerned that they would lose the tons of supplies in Philadelphia if the British captured the city, began dispersing them to more secure premises. Unfortunately for Dewees, Valley Forge was one of the spots selected. Dewees justifiably feared that accepting the supplies was tantamount to painting huge bull's-eyes on

Dewees's house at Valley Forge.

all his buildings, but probably feeling that he had little choice in the matter, he complied with the request, and the next day tons of commissary stores were brought to him.

On September 18, Dewees's fears were realized when a party of British dragoons swooped down on Valley Forge. At the time, a handful of Americans—including Dewees; Alexander Hamilton, the future first secretary of the treasury of the United States; and "Light Horse" Harry Lee, a future governor of Virginia and father of Robert E. Lee—were in the process of removing supplies. Shots were fired, and Dewees and Hamilton escaped by crossing the Schuylkill River on a boat, while Lee, trusting to the speed of his horse, sped west on present-day Route 23, eventually leaving the British in his dust.

That night, the British took possession of the property, and three days later, they set fire to everything they couldn't carry and marched off. Dewees's loss included the forge, the sawmill, two large stone houses and four hundred loads of coal, as well as all of his supplies, livestock and belongings.

However, Dewees's problems were just beginning. On October 24, Dewees, also a colonel in the Pennsylvania militia, in company with another man, was captured by the British and imprisoned in Philadelphia for three and a half days "without a morsel of any kind of provision." Their captors eventually freed them, but while in jail their rations were meager. Finally, to avoid starvation, they earned their release by taking an oath of allegiance to King George III.

The final act in Dewees's tragedy began on December 19 when the Continental army moved into its winter camps, which included much of his property at Valley Forge. The Americans, in need of shelter and warmth, burned all of Dewees's fence rails and cut down all of his remaining trees. The loss forced the man into bankruptcy in 1784.

A year later, Dewees petitioned Congress for compensation, stating that "a merciless enemy" had "either carried off or burned" his property and that the American soldiers' destruction of the "greatest part of his standing timber and all of his fences deprived [him] of the power to erect New Buildings and rendered the Premises of less Value than they previously were."

It is believed that Dewees died about 1809. Congress never acted on his petition during his life. In 1818, President James Madison signed a petition granting $8,000 in relief to Dewees's widow for damages inflicted by the British, but Congress would not act on the claim for the damages caused by the American soldiers.

JONATHAN POTTS THE REBEL AND JOHN POTTS THE TORY

Two Brothers in America's First Civil War

Although most Americans supported the War for Independence, there were an estimated 75,000 to 100,000 who opposed it because they wanted to remain British citizens. These Loyalists, or Tories, came from all levels of society, from the wealthy and the powerful to mechanics and farmers. They often demonstrated the strength of their conviction by fighting for what they felt was their proper government, and because they lived in all of the colonies, sometimes neighbor was pitted against neighbor, friend against friend and kinsman against kinsman. Thus, the Revolutionary War was a civil war of a very personal nature, and the stakes were high because most of the losers would not be allowed to go home in peace.

The family of Pottstown's founder, John Potts Sr., provides an illustration of what happened when brothers chose different sides. Almost all of the Potts family supported the American Revolution in many ways. They manufactured cannons and ordnance, they helped raise money, they were on committees and they served in the army. When the Revolution ended, most of them, despite financial losses, got on with their lives.

The war destroyed two of them. Jonathan Potts, one of the many sons of John Potts, was born on April 11, 1745, while the family lived at Popodickon, the Potts home just west of Boyertown. He studied medicine in Edinburgh, Scotland, and received his doctorate from the Academy and College of Philadelphia, now the University of Pennsylvania, in 1771. He began practicing medicine in Reading, Pennsylvania.

Dr. Potts was an early and zealous activist for the cause of independence. In 1775, he served in Pennsylvania's Provisional Congress. He was also very active in raising and organizing the local militia and, for a while in 1776, was an officer in one the Berks County militia battalions.

In April of 1776, Congress appointed him director of hospitals in Canada, and then in June, he was appointed to the same post for Lake George in upper New York. Initially, the war did not go well for the American forces in the north. Dr. Potts reported from Fort Ticonderoga on July 16, 1776:

> I went to Crown Point...found the wretched remains of what was once a very respectable body of troops—that pestilential disease the small pox has taken such deep root that the Camp has more the appearance of a General Hospital than an army.

In December of that year, at the request of George Washington, Potts went to Philadelphia. But by the spring of 1777, he had traveled back north to Albany, New York, where he served as the director of hospitals in the Northern Department.

On November 6, 1777, the federal Congress passed a resolution praising Potts and his medical staff for their "unremitted attention shown...to the sick and wounded under their charge." Potts was then appointed director general of hospitals in the Middle Department and was at the Continental army's Valley Forge encampment during the brutal winter of 1777–78.

John Potts Jr., the Tory.

Under the constant strain of travel, exposure and caring for the sick and wounded, Jonathan Potts's health failed, forcing him to return to Reading. In a letter he wrote in April 1780 to the chairman of the medical committee, Potts declared, "My indisposition of my body contracted in your service prevents me from…the execution of my office." But even though his body had failed, his spirit was still strong. He continued, "I shall at all times be ready (if I can but crawl) to contribute my might towards the full & final establishment of our glorious independence."

Jonathan Potts died at his home in Reading in October 1781 without seeing the "final establishment" of America's "glorious independence." His body was brought back to Pottstown and buried at the family cemetery. Being a Quaker, his grave was unmarked. In the 1850s, one of his grandsons wanted to place a small marker on his burial site. It is only fitting that the then-ancient Jacob Drinkhouse, Pottstown's last surviving Revolutionary War veteran, was the man who pointed out the spot where Jonathan Potts lay.

John Potts Jr., the third son of John Potts Sr. and an older brother of Jonathan, was born at Colebrook Dale Furnace on October 15, 1738. A graduate of the Academy and College of Philadelphia, Potts also studied law in London, but even though he earned a license to practice in Philadelphia, he primarily worked in the Potts family iron business.

By 1775, John Potts was a wealthy and politically influential businessman. In addition to his iron forges, he had many investments in Philadelphia and was also a justice of the peace for Philadelphia County and judge on the Court of Common Pleas for Philadelphia County and City. Along with his substantial home in Philadelphia, John Potts owned one in Pottstown and a spacious country house, called Stowe, on 275 acres just west of town.

However, when the rebellion cauldron began to bubble, Potts, whose pro-British stance was well known, began to feel the heat. He wrote later that "when the inhabitants [of Philadelphia] were arming," he had made himself "obnoxious by disapproving of their conduct." So he prudently left the city for his country estate, where he could keep a lower profile.

While living in the Pottstown area, Potts, in the face of spreading revolutionary zeal there, "fervently exerted himself...to prevent the progress of these discontents." This stance again "rendered him obnoxious" and caused "frequent attempts" to be "made by bodies of armed men to apprehend [him]."

With the British invasion of southeastern Pennsylvania in September 1777, the war really heated up, so Potts's Loyalist sympathies forced him to flee back to Philadelphia, which was now safe for him because the British controlled it. He had to leave Pottstown so quickly that his wife, Margaret, and their three children were temporarily left behind. In December, Potts had the nerve to visit the American encampment at Valley Forge and petition George Washington for permission for his family to join him in the city. In a letter of December 20, Washington stated, "When Mrs. Potts applies she will have my permission for herself and Children to go into Philadelphia."

But there was no haven for Potts. When the British evacuated Philadelphia in June 1778, he was forced to follow them to New York City, and when they left that place in 1783, there was no safe place in the American colonies for him.

When the war ended, the British government offered land in Nova Scotia to loyal colonists. That is where John Potts and at least one of his sons went. But despite his failure to back the Revolution, Potts, like most Tories, still thought of himself as an American and wanted to return to his homeland.

John Potts's home at High and Hanover Streets is shown here in a photograph from the first decade of the twentieth century. *Courtesy of the Pottstown Historical Society.*

In 1786, the Potts family's political influence proved strong enough to win the wayward son a pardon. But he paid a fearful price for supporting the losing side. All of his personal and real property was confiscated. His wife had died in New York City. Of his three children, his sons, Stephen and Samuel, served in the military forces of Great Britain but later returned to the United States, while his daughter, Mary Ann, who was born in Philadelphia in 1768, married David Rutter, the iron master at nearby Pine Forge.

After his return to his native country, Potts disappeared, and to this day, no one knows what happened to him. For a scion of a wealthy and powerful family who kept detailed records of their members, this unknown end is an anomaly. It is as if the stigma of his political leanings placed him in a limbo from which he will never return.

As for Potts's forfeited property in the Pottstown area, Stowe, his country estate, was rented by his brother Samuel. According to Daniel Graham, well-known historian of the colonial iron industry, "The farm was eventually sold and the property subdivided and developed but the house was in existence up until at least 1924."

In 1780, Arthur St. Clair, a general in the American army during the Revolutionary War, purchased Potts's house at the southeast corner of High and Hanover Streets. It is doubtful that St. Clair spent much time in Pottstown, but because he was a Revolutionary War hero and the president of the Continental Congress in 1787, the Schuylkill Valley Chapter of the Daughters of the American Revolution placed a bronze marker on the house. (It is still there.) In 1909, and probably from that time, everybody in the area referred to the building as the General St. Clair Mansion.

Potts's house was demolished in 1924 and replaced with the three-story commercial building that still stands on the spot. Even though the house was destroyed, it did, in the style of the phoenix, rise again from its ashes. William H. Wiand, the contractor who razed it, loved its red sandstone blocks that had been quarried 160 years earlier, so he had them split and redressed and used them to build a home for his family at 370 North York Street. According to the *Pottstown News* of December 1, 1926, Wiand and his family had just moved into the house, which he named St. Clair. It stands today, a link to John Potts's ruin almost 230 years ago.

Part II

POTTSTOWN IN THE NINETEENTH CENTURY

Glimpses of Life

———•———

FROM MUDDY ROADS TO RAILROADS

Better Transportation Drives Pottstown's Growth

In December 1761, John Potts, a marvelously gifted and successful colonial businessman, was advertising building lots for sale in Pottsgrove, a new town he was developing. To potential buyers, Potts touted his town as being "admirably suited for commerce" because it was located "on the River Schuylkill," and two "very public and Great Road[s]" intersected there.

By modern standards, there were no "Great Roads" in colonial America. Even the best of them were nothing but narrow ribbons of dirt that, when dry, were covered in ankle-deep dust and laced with bone-jarring, axle-breaking ruts and, when wet, were impassable quagmires. The Reverend Henry Muhlenberg, a well-known colonial-era Lutheran minister, wrote about the hardships of traveling on the Great Road from Reading to Pottstown: "The road was rocky and steep, and also slippery…Under God's gracious protection we covered nine miles over this bad road in [four hours]."

The roads were so bad that freight was shipped on the Schuylkill River when the water was high enough, which was not very often. Running freight on the river gave rise to the Reading boat; long, narrow and "sharp at both ends," it could carry loads as heavy as one hundred barrels of flour, required a three- to five-man crew, didn't draw much water and was easy to handle. Propelled by the racing current, the boats could quickly travel from Pottstown to Philadelphia. John Thompson, an early Pottstown burgess, worked on one as a teenager and remembered that if the water was really high, they could make the city in about twelve hours. Although the downstream run could be fast and exciting, the return trip against the current was an arduous one that, even with a light cargo, took a good five days and required every man to push with a steel-tipped pole every inch of the way.

The first road improvements in the Pottstown area came between 1811 and 1815 when a group of investors formed the Perkiomen and Ridge Turnpike Company and improved the twenty-nine-mile section of what is now Ridge Pike from Collegeville to Reading. In February 1826, a young engineer from Virginia traveled this stretch of road and wrote to his father:

> *The turnpike over which we passed was tolerable. It may be called very good considering…the great travel on it, and the bad weather…It seems to be made mostly of limestone in fragments which seems to have sunk one layer after another* [like] *the McAdam roads of England do.*

In Pottstown (which then only stretched from Adams Street on the east to the Manatawny Creek on the west), the turnpike was a forty-foot-wide strip that ran right down the middle of High Street, which, per John Potts's order, was one hundred feet wide. A man who grew up in town in the 1820s later recalled that for years people walked on "a footpath…and the space between the path and the turnpike was sod, which furnished pasture for numerous flocks of geese that had had the privilege of roaming at large." There were also several streams that ran south through town, cutting across High Street. The turnpike company bridged these runs along its right of way, but the borough did nothing along its parts, so pedestrians had to cross them by walking on makeshift bridges consisting of a couple of wooden planks.

Hard on the heels of the Perkiomen Turnpike came the Schuylkill Navigation System, a series of canals and dams built by the Schuylkill Navigation Company. Upon its completion in 1823, it was possible to ship anything that would fit into a canalboat along the system's entire 108-mile length from Port Carbon to Philadelphia. The harnessing of

A canalboat passing through Laurel Locks. *Courtesy of the Pottstown Historical Society.*

the river's resources created a water route that was far superior to that of the roads or the river and made the canal system the undisputed king of freight transportation.

In the Pottstown area, the canal was on the south side of the river, so it bypassed Pottstown. Nevertheless, it helped the development of business in the borough by making it cheaper and easier for merchants and local manufacturers to ship and buy goods.

Today, when it is possible to fly thousands of miles in less time than it took a canalboat to travel from Pottsville to Philadelphia, the canals seem quaint. However, to people living in the Schuylkill Valley at the time, the Schuylkill Navigation System was astounding. This is shown by the excitement that the opening generated in Pottstown. On July 7, 1824, the *Pottstown Times* reported that on July 5 "we had the pleasure of visiting the Schuylkill Canal at Laurel Hill…That day being set apart by the managers…to test the canal" by taking two boats from Reading to Philadelphia.

Many people from Pottstown, enthused about the opening ceremonies, paraded all the way to Laurel Locks accompanied by the town's militia company, which took with it a cannon to salute the boats "with a discharge of musketry and a field piece." The paper noted that "upwards of a thousand people [certainly not all from Pottstown] attended to see this novel scene of boats passing through the locks."

When the ceremony ended, the Pottstown contingent went back to town, where "Capt. Burns had an elegant repast for them...on the Schuylkill a few yards above the [Hanover Street] bridge." Burns had a distillery, and during the course of the "elegant repast," the guests drank fourteen toasts, "after which they marched into town making a great parade, the Union Guards in full uniform and the citizens bringing up the rear, each with a branch of white poplar bearing up in his hand." It seems that despite the fourteen toasts, the procession marched through town with "that decorum and hilarity becoming the day," and eventually everybody "retired with peace and satisfaction each to his respective home."

The canal's greatest period of prosperity was from 1835 to 1841. Following that, profits declined due to competition from the Philadelphia and Reading Railroad (P&R), and by 1870, the Schuylkill Navigation System was no longer viable and was rented by the same railroad that had ruined it. After this, the amount of traffic on the canal steadily declined until, by the beginning of the twentieth century, there was almost none. It lingered

The Philadelphia and Reading's passenger station shown here was replaced in 1928. *Courtesy of the Pottstown Historical Society.*

for years in an increasing state of neglect, and in 1949, it was given to the Commonwealth of Pennsylvania.

Construction on the railroad began in 1837, and by December of that year, the line was open from Pottstown to Reading. Two years later, the P&R's service was complete from Reading to Philadelphia, and on January 1, 1842, the last link in its chain was forged when a train ran over the entire line from Mount Carbon, near Pottsville, to Philadelphia.

The railroad gave Pottstown's economy an immediate boost by opening in town a blacksmith and a machine shop and, later, its car shops, which were the center of all of its car building and repair work. This latter operation was so large that it occupied the entire block between South, Penn, Queen and Charlotte Streets. The first iron truss bridge used in North America was built in that blacksmith shop. One of its girders eventually found its way to the Smithsonian Institution in Washington, D.C.

The railroad was by far the most important factor in Pottstown's future growth and economic prosperity. With its rails all but impervious to bad weather and its steam engines capable of transporting tons of freight, it provided, for the first time, dependable, fast and economical transportation that linked Pottstown not just to local markets but also, over time, to the entire world. By 1850, the town's population had more than doubled from 721 to 1,664, and ten years later it had expanded to 2,380. This increase was due to the rapid growth of industry that followed the railroad's appearance.

THE CIVIL WAR

Pottstown Answers the Union's Call

The Civil War is the most studied event in America's history. Over the years, countless thousands of books have been devoted to the war's battles and important leaders, but the stories of the millions of average people who were caught up in the violence, stress and uncertainty of the early 1860s are just as compelling and also deserve to be told. The people of the Pottstown area supported the Union war effort, and many men from the

A photo from the Mexican War era of Andrew H. Tippin, later colonel of the Sixty-eighth Pennsylvania Infantry during the Civil War, and his wife, Ellen Lightcap. *Courtesy of the Pottstown Historical Society.*

area served in the Federal armed forces. The following are a few vignettes about their experiences.

In August 1862, Pottstown resident Frank Wildermuth walked into the basement of the Madison Hotel on High Street and joined an infantry company that would become part of the Sixty-eighth Pennsylvania

Volunteers. Less than a year later, on July 2, 1863, Wildermuth was wounded while fighting in John Sherfy's Peach Orchard during the Battle of Gettysburg. In the smoke and confusion of the mêlée, he disappeared and was never seen or heard from again. Many years later, Wildermuth's old comrades theorized that he had gone into Sherfy's barn for shelter and died there when it burned the next day after being hit by artillery shells. A few days after the battle, a graphic description of Wildermuth's end was provided by a member of the Seventy-seventh New York who wrote to his wife that in the barn's ruins he saw "crisped and blackened limbs, heads and other portions of bodies lying half consumed among the heaps and ashes"; even to this combat-hardened veteran, it was "one of the most ghastly pictures ever witnessed."

Wildermuth's regiment, the Sixty-eighth Pennsylvania Volunteer Infantry, was commanded by Andrew Hart Tippin, a man with very strong ties to Pottstown. Born on Christmas Day 1823 in Plymouth Township, Montgomery County, Pennsylvania, Tippin came to Pottstown in 1845 when he became half owner of the *Berks Chester and Montgomery Ledger*, Pottstown's weekly newspaper. A year later, his ties to the community were further strengthened by his marriage to Pottstown resident Miss Ellen Lightcap. He served with the Eleventh U.S. Infantry during the war with Mexico and was brevetted twice for gallant and meritorious conduct in battle. After the war, he returned to Pottstown, where he lived until 1857, when he moved to Philadelphia.

When the Civil War began, Tippin was appointed a major in a ninety-day regiment, and in 1862, he was commissioned a colonel and given command of a three-year regiment. Tippin's new command, the Sixty-eighth, was recruited primarily from Philadelphia, but his popularity in Pottstown made it possible to recruit company H, about one hundred men, from this area. Tippin remained in command of the regiment until it was mustered out in June 1865. In February 1870, Tippin died from an episode of chronic dysentery, a disease he picked up in Mexico. He is buried in the eastern section of Pottstown Cemetery.

Pottstown resident William Price Bach also enlisted in Company H. Like Frank Wildermuth, he came to grief in the Peach Orchard at Gettysburg, where he was hit in the right foot by a piece of artillery shell and then in the left leg by a musket ball. Completely helpless, Bach lay on the field while Confederate troops streamed by him. In 1903, Bach recounted that at one point a Rebel sergeant thrust a bayonet within six inches of his face and threatened to "finish" him. Thinking fast, Bach told the man, "Hold on. I'm shot through both legs." The Reb reluctantly agreed that Bach "wouldn't do

A Civil War veteran from Pottstown wearing his GAR uniform. *Courtesy of the author.*

any more damage" and went on his way. Poor Bach was finally rescued by Union soldiers on the night of July 3 and received medical attention.

Eventually, the surgeons removed thirty-five pieces of bone from Bach's right leg, forcing him to wear a steel leg brace for the rest of his life, but this didn't stop him from living life to the fullest. He returned to Pottstown upon his discharge, went back to his trade as a harness and saddle maker and, two years later, married Elisabeth May. The couple eventually had seven children. Bach was also very active in civic affairs, serving as president of the school board and as Pottstown's burgess. He died on February 1, 1920, and is buried in the eastern section of Pottstown Cemetery.

The Fifty-third Pennsylvania Volunteer Infantry was one of the Army of the Potomac's elite combat regiments. During the war, it fought in twenty-three battles and numerous skirmishes, from the Battle of Seven Pines on June 1, 1862, until the surrender of the Army of Northern Virginia at Appomattox Court House on April 9, 1865.

An entire company of that regiment was recruited in Pottstown. Amazingly, a few of its members somehow managed to come through the war unscathed by disease or battle. One was William Mintzer, whose home stood on what is now a parking lot for Holy Trinity Roman Catholic Church. Mintzer served more than four years and rose in rank from a private to a colonel with a brevet of brigadier general. Born on June 3, 1837, in North Coventry Township, Chester County, Mintzer died on March 31, 1916, and is buried at Edgewood Cemetery.

The two Graham brothers, also members of the Fifty-third, were not as fortunate as Mintzer. Eli Graham, who was mortally wounded on June 1, 1861, at the Battle of Seven Pines, has the melancholy distinction of being the first man from Pottstown killed in combat during the war. Shortly after his death, his brother, William, wrote to his parents, "Eli is dead and it is so lonesome without him, but it is God's will and we must submit." A little more than two years later, on June 3, 1864, the Graham family again had to "submit to God's will" when William was mortally wounded at the Battle of Cold Harbor, less than ten miles from where Eli was killed. In the eastern section of the Pottstown Cemetery, there is a much-weathered tombstone bearing the names of the Graham brothers, but their remains are in Virginia. Eli's remains rest in the small national cemetery that marks the Seven Pines battlefield, and William's are probably buried in an unmarked grave somewhere in the vicinity of Cold Harbor.

After the war the surviving veterans had to get on with their lives. Some came home to Pottstown to stay, while others moved on. Over the years, those who stayed were joined by a large number who came to town looking for better opportunities. As the years passed, the "stayers" and the "comers," united by their shared war experiences, banded together to relive those war years and to take steps to see that what they and their fallen comrades had accomplished would not be forgotten.

To this end, they formed the Eli Graham and the Mark Edgar Richards GAR (Grand Army of the Republic) Posts. (The GAR was the Civil War veteran's equivalent of today's American Legion and developed into a powerful lobby that was influential in national and state politics.) The posts had monthly meetings and suppers where members spun yarns about their war experiences, performed skits, recited poems or sang songs. In 1909, the *Pottstown Ledger* mentioned a meeting of the Union Veteran Legion that adjourned to Schwab's "refreshment parlor," where its members had a "good time eating ice cream and other good things" while they told stories. At some point, "Squire Neiman [Jonathan Neiman of the Sixty-eighth Pennsylvania], pressed to sing some of the old songs," came through with "The Sword of Bunker Hill," "Paradise

The GAR Statue in its original spot at High and Charlotte Streets. *Courtesy of the Pottstown Historical Society.*

Alley" and "Over the Hill to the Poor House." For his efforts, Neiman was "applauded to the echo."

In 1879, the Graham GAR Post bought a large lot in the eastern section of the Pottstown Cemetery for the use of veterans and placed on it a large obelisk with the names of deceased soldiers from town inscribed on the four sides of its base. The monument was dedicated on July 4 with an artillery salute at dawn followed at noon by a large parade that included fifteen hundred veterans from all over southeastern Pennsylvania.

A familiar sight in Pottstown today is the GAR Statue, a Civil War memorial that came to town in 1893. It was a gift from Miss Annie Richards to the M.E. Richards GAR Post in memory of her late brother, Mathias Edgar Richards, who served as major of the Ninety-sixth Pennsylvania and then as a staff officer in the Army of the Potomac. The monument consists of a bronze statue of a Civil War soldier standing on top of an eight-foot-tall base. Its unique feature was inside the base, where water pipes fed multiple drinking "basins" to cater to the thirst of man, horse and dog. It was placed at the northwest corner of High and Charlotte

John B. Boyer, Pottstown's, and all of Montgomery County's, last surviving veteran of the Civil War. *Courtesy of Robert Eppehimer.*

Streets in front of Dr. Mark Withers's drugstore, because Withers, also a Civil War veteran, had a good artesian well to tap into. After a century of weathering the elements, the GAR Statue was beginning to show signs of wear and tear, so in 1994 it was given a face-lift that restored its bright bronze finish. Today, it stands watch on the north side of High Street between Evans and Franklin.

With the passing of the years, the veterans' ranks slowly thinned until only one remained—John B. Boyer. Born in 1841 in New Hanover Township, just north of Pottstown, Boyer came through many battles without a scratch. After the war, he came to town, where he worked as a blacksmith in several of Pottstown's ironworks and retired in 1926 at the age of eighty-five. Boyer died at his home, 227 Beech Street, on February 7, 1938, making him the last surviving Civil War veteran in Montgomery County. He was a child when the United States went to war with Mexico in 1847, and had he lived another eighteen months, he would have seen the beginning of World War II.

MAJOR GENERAL JOHN RUTTER BROOKE

From Farm Boy to General

John Brooke, the son of William Brooke and his wife, Martha Rutter, was born on July 19, 1838, on his parents' farm near the mouth of Sprogel's Run in what is now Lower Pottsgrove Township. Brooke would go on to become a major general in the United States Army, but his military career, rather than commencing at West Point, began almost by accident with the start of the Civil War in April 1861, when the Pottstown militia company, known as the Madison Guards, enlisted to serve for ninety days. The men asked Brooke to be their captain when their regular commander resigned only two days before the company was to report for duty because his new bride became "violently hysterical" when she learned that he would be "going off to war." Fear for her sanity forced him to step down.

Despite his youth and lack of formal military training, Brooke did an excellent job performing his duties as company commander. A Pottstown man who was a member of the company wrote:

> *There is something about him* [Brooke] *that may be termed the "art Napoleon—the mystery of command"…kind yet firm—free and easy with the men, yet in all his associations with us there is something about the man that forces us to acknowledge his authority and submit to his superior position.*

The company's term of enlistment expired on July 20, 1861, one day before the Battle of First Manassas. However, the desire of many of Brooke's men to fight still flowed unabated, as John Brooke noted in a letter to his father: "We will all come home to see you once more… [but] we will come out again in a different organization, all our boys are anxious and willing for the time to come when…they shall again be upon the warpath."

In July, Brooke received a colonel's commission from Pennsylvania's governor, Andrew Curtin. The boy captain was now a boy colonel, in charge

John Rutter Brooke as major general of volunteers in the Civil War. *Courtesy of the United States Army Military History Institute.*

of an entire regiment of infantry, which, at full strength, numbered one thousand men. Because of Brooke's popularity, an entire company—one hundred men—was recruited from the Pottstown area to serve for three years in the newly minted colonel's outfit. In August, the men boarded the train for Camp Curtin in Harrisburg, and in November, they journeyed to Washington, D.C. As part of the Fifty-third Pennsylvania Volunteer Infantry, they were officially accepted into the Army of the Potomac.

The Fifty-third's first taste of combat came on June 1, 1862, during the Battle of Seven Pines, a two-day affair fought seven miles east of Richmond. There was no fancy maneuvering in this engagement. The fighting was simple and brutal: two lines of infantry blazed away at each other at a distance of about one hundred yards. An officer leading his men from the front was taking a terrible risk, but Brooke was more than equal to the task. Samuel Hockley Rutter, a first cousin of Brooke, described his kinsman's performance in a letter to his mother: "Oh mother! You should have seen Col. Brooke going ahead of the regiment with his sword drawn and saying

'Come on Boys!' He used to tell us to lie down, while he stood up, the bullets whistling around him."

Brooke's conduct was also noted by his brigade commander, General William French, a hard-boiled regular army officer who was not easily impressed: "For some time the most desperate efforts were made to break our lines. The left of the 53rd Pa…led by the gallant Colonel Brooke, repulsed them, again and again."

During the next two years, John Brooke fought in almost every battle in which the Army of the Potomac was engaged, and in all of these he exposed himself as recklessly as he had in his first. At the Battle of Fredericksburg on December 13, 1862, Brooke led the Fifty-third in an attack on Mayre's Heights, where the Confederates, protected by a stone wall, slaughtered Union soldiers who had to cross about six hundred yards of open ground to reach them. John Brooke took his men closer to that stone wall than any other Union regiment. Levi Fritz, from Pottstown, a member of Company A, described the experience: "Up this hill, the open door to death our troops must needs go…Col. Brooke shows them the way, leads them on through the rain of bullets and artillery shells." General Samuel Zook, Brooke's brigade commander, wrote, "Col. John R. Brooke, with this gallant regiment, the 53rd Pa, from being unhurt, was enabled to perform the biggest service to his country, and added to the laurels he and his regiment had already won on many fields of honor."

At Gettysburg on the afternoon of July 2, Brooke, now commanding a brigade, took part in a Union counterattack that drove the Confederates from the wheat field. Brooke provided the impetus that got the Union line moving. Harry Pfanz, a noted Gettysburg historian, wrote in his book *Gettysburg the Second Day*:

> *It was a gallant charge, one of the few made by troops of the Army of the Potomac, and it required some leadership. At one point Brooke restored momentum by seizing the colors of the Fifty-third Pennsylvania and leading the way with them.*

Again, Brooke's conduct during the battle won the praise of his superior officer. Brigadier General John Caldwell, his division commander, wrote, "Of the merit of Colonel Brooke…too much can scarcely be said."

Brooke was wounded four times during the war; the last, serious enough to end his role as a combat commander, was on June 3, 1864, during the Battle of Cold Harbor. He was hit in the arm and side by pieces of an

John Rutter Brooke as a major general in the United States Army, 1897. *Courtesy of the United States Army Military History Institute.*

artillery shell. He later was promoted to brigadier general to date from May 12, 1864, and on August 1, 1864, he was awarded by brevet the rank of major general for gallantry at Totopotomoy and Cold Harbor.

But even during war, there was time for romance. On the day before Christmas 1863, the young colonel married Miss Louisa Roberts of Chester County. According to a later newspaper account, "She was one of the most noted beauties of the region…The people who remember her speak with a sigh of her beauty of face and loveliness of nature."

Brooke resigned from the army on January 24, 1866, and returned home to his wife and baby son. However, he couldn't resist the siren call of military life. Less than nine months later, he accepted an appointment as a lieutenant colonel in the Thirty-seventh Infantry and reported for active duty at Fort Union, New Mexico, in August 1867.

Because Louisa Brooke was pregnant, she remained behind at his father's home. When Brooke left, it probably didn't occur to him that he would never see her again, but two months later she died giving birth to their second son.

Her husband, who was stationed two thousand miles away, couldn't even come home in time for the funeral.

Brooke remained a widower for the next ten years. Then, in 1877, he married Mary Stearns, daughter of Onslow Stearns, a former governor of New Hampshire. The intrepid Mary accompanied Brooke to all of his posts. In 1899, she recalled that her "wedding journey was a 688 mile march away from the nearest rail road," and she then spent "3 months living in tents in the cold northwest."

During Brooke's second term of service, he had twenty assignments, ranging from the bleak frontier to Chicago and New York City. He always performed his duties skillfully and lobbied tenaciously for his promotions, which came slowly in the peacetime army.

In 1898, Brooke was finally promoted to the rank of major general, and with the outbreak of the Spanish-American War, he was made commander of the first army corps. In October of that year, he was appointed military governor of Puerto Rico and, two months later, was named military governor of Cuba, a post he held for one year.

Naturally, a high-profile post like this would attract a lot of newspaper coverage. It is interesting that in an article in the *New York Herald*, an officer who served with Brooke was quoted as saying, "On account of a strong personal magnetism, he was popular with staff officers as well as those who came to know him." These words are remarkably similar to those written about him thirty-seven years earlier by the Pottstonian who served under him in the early days of the Civil War.

Brooke retired from the army in 1902 to a home he had built in Rosemont, Montgomery County, Pennsylvania. In April of that year, his name was mentioned as a possible "compromise candidate" for the Republican nomination for governor of Pennsylvania. Some of the veterans who had served under him during the Spanish-American War endorsed him, stating, "He endeared himself to the hearts of all the soldiers of his command, and demonstrated his splendid executive ability, both military and civilian." However, this came to naught, and the old soldier spent most of his remaining time traveling. He died at the Friend's Asylum in the Frankfort section of Philadelphia on September 5, 1926, and is buried at Arlington Cemetery.

POTTSTOWN'S FIRE COMPANIES

The Boys Who Ran with the Machine

Before the existence of volunteer fire companies in Pottstown, fires were fought by ad hoc bucket brigades. In the 1830s, Pottstown's borough council took its first step in assuming municipal responsibility for fighting fires by buying the Pilot, a crude apparatus with a wooden water tank less than three feet high, mounted on four wheels and pulled to fires by citizens. Once there, the arms of citizens provided the power that pumped water on the blaze, while others brought buckets of water to keep the tank filled.

In the 1850s, the council upgraded to the Madison, which, although requiring hand pumping and towing, had the ability to suck water from a source such as a well or creek. In May 1860, the *Ledger* reported that the Madison was "speedily" put to use when "some rascally incendiary" set fire to a hayrick on the premises of General James Rittenhouse, which conveniently was located very close to Manatawny Creek. (Rittenhouse's property ran along the east side of Manatawny Street for about half a block between High and King.)

The torching of the hayrick was a mere nuisance in comparison with fires later in the decade. In July 1868, a conflagration destroyed several buildings of the Pottstown Iron Company and some of the adjoining private homes. With many men put temporarily out of work, the need for an organized fire company was strongly felt. The last barrier to this was removed in 1870, when the Pottstown Gas and Water Company laid its pipes under the town's streets and installed fire hydrants.

In December, the borough council bought one thousand feet of leather fire hose and a hose cart from the Philadelphia Fire Company No. 18. Less than a month later, on January 3, 1871, a town meeting was held in which a fire company was organized. A long and heated discussion of what to name it resulted in Pottstown quickly gaining another one.

A "large majority of those present" voted to use the name Philadelphia; after all, it was already painted on both sides of the hose cart. Others favored Goodwill—as in "goodwill to all"—and when they lost the election, they organized the Goodwill Fire Company three days later.

The next day, the Phillies got the hose and cart from the borough council, but apart from the ineffectual Madison, neither company as yet had a

Trucks of the Philadelphia Fire Company in the early 1950s. *Courtesy of the Krause Collection.*

firefighting apparatus. However, that was not perceived as a problem. It would only be necessary to attach the hose to one of the new hydrants, and the pressure in the water company's lines would be enough to "play the water stream on the fire." Unfortunately, the pressure sometimes was inadequate—one issue of the *Ledger* reported that dirt and mud from one hydrant clogged the fire hoses—so by mid-1871, both companies had raised the money to buy a pumper that used steam power to create enough pressure to deliver the water.

The Philadelphia Steam Fire Engine Company No. 1 immediately set up quarters in a building on the south side of King Street between Hanover and York. In June 1880, the company moved to the quarters it still occupies at the southeast corner of Chestnut and Penn Streets. The construction work on this building was done almost entirely by members, who volunteered their time and expertise. For instance, the masonry and brickwork were done by and under the supervision of Thomas Yergey, who served in the Sixth Pennsylvania Cavalry during the Civil War and was famous in Pottstown as a bricklayer and father of twenty children.

The Goodwill Steam and Fire Engine Company No.1 had its first engine house in a building located on King Street between Hanover and York, and in 1882, it began constructing a new engine house at 28 South Hanover. The building, which still stands, was formally dedicated on May 20, 1883. It

Early equipment of the Goodwill Fire Company. *Courtesy of the Pottstown Historical Society.*

was a proud day for Goodwill members, marked by a large firemen's parade, formal speeches and a party at the new engine house.

In 1889, even though Pottstown did not have a hospital, the need for an ambulance was felt; the *Ledger* reported, "The town has a use for just such a wagon almost every day of the week." The Goodwill Fire Company provided the service, and its first ambulance, which was built at Van Buskirk's carriage works, had a "glistening dark body bearing 'Goodwill Ambulance' on both sides and wheels and running gear of red with yellow trimming." It made its debut on March 29, being "driven about the town for the citizens' approval." To make it accessible, a telephone was installed at the engine house, and Sylvester Missimer was hired as the driver. The cost of setting up the operation—including the stretcher and "other furnishings"—was $300, paid for in part by donations.

An examination of the Pottstown newspaper revealed that Missimer's first call came on April 11, when he was summoned to the Sotter Boiler Works (then located on Beech Street between York and Hanover) to carry Ben Kalis

An early machine of the Empire Hook and Ladder Company. *Courtesy of the Pottstown Historical Society.*

to his home because he suffered a "series of severe gashes over his left eye and some deep bruises and cuts on his arms."

The Goodwill's dual role as an ambulance service and fire company created a need for more space. In 1954, it bought the Henry J. Snyder home at 700 High Street. Eventually, that building was razed and the company's new facilities were built on that site.

As Pottstown grew, residents of what was then the east end of town felt a need for a fire company in their neighborhood. On July 18, 1876, they formed the Sunrise (now the Empire) Hook and Ladder Company. The company's first engine house was at 431 High Street, and on July 4, 1885, the company's present headquarters, at the northeast corner of Chestnut and Franklin Streets, was formally dedicated.

In the first years of the Pottstown fire companies, members literally pulled their machines to a fire. It is hard to imagine men straining to pull a ton of wood and iron mounted on narrow, iron-rimmed wheels through the town's muddy streets, where every little grade was a major obstacle.

Washington S. Royer, a former Pottstown burgess who ran with the machine in his younger days, described the process:

Pottstown in the Nineteenth Century

There was a friendly rivalry among the boys as to who would secure the honor of manning the tongue of the carriage...they would reel out the rope as more recruits arrived until at times thirty or forty men urging each other on with lusty cries were struggling to get to the scene of the fire as soon as possible.

Between 1885 and 1888, all of the Pottstown fire companies switched to horses to pull their equipment. For example, in 1885 the Philadelphia Fire Company bought two horses whose total weight was 2,900 pounds. They were "just what were wanted to carry the Silsby steamer (which weighed about 5,000 pounds) in a jiffy." Over the years, the process for assembling the team and leaving the building became faster.

Danny Weidner, who drove a team for the Phillies for twenty years, described how the horses would be brought from the stable and would stand perfectly still as the harnesses were quickly lowered on them and, with a "few snaps, were ready to go." By 1889, the doors opened electrically, and as the team dashed from the engine room, a gas-fed fire in the floor flared up through the grates of the engine's boiler, igniting wood shavings, which in turn kindled the soft coal. Before the engine left the house, "flames were rearing from the top of the stack," and within a block, the boiler had steam. The exciting spectacle of two powerful horses careering at full tilt through the town's old streets with smoke and flames shooting from the boiler's brass smokestack brought "persons from squares to see them pass."

In the years following World War II, hundreds of new homes were built in the north end of Pottstown, creating a need for another fire company. On January 14, 1950, a group of north end residents met at Brook Side Country Club and laid the foundation for what would become the North End Fire Company at 301 Prospect Street.

During the second decade of the twentieth century, all of the Pottstown companies switched to trucks propelled with internal combustion engines. At present, the four companies operate under the command of a borough fire chief. Between them, they have twelve pieces of firefighting and rescue equipment. Each company has professionally trained engine drivers on duty around the clock for faster response time and receives a yearly contribution from the borough, but all rely heavily on fundraising projects to meet their rising expenses.

———◆———

TROLLEYS SPEED UP LIFE IN POTTSTOWN

In the decades following the Civil War, the continued growth of railroads in America made it possible to cross the continent in a matter of days or travel to the next station in twenty minutes, but once beyond the railroad's network, people still had to travel over bad roads by horse or on foot the same way Americans did at the beginning of the nineteenth century.

An excellent solution to this local travel problem came in 1888 when the first electric streetcar system, designed by engineer/inventor Frank J. Sprague, began to operate in Richmond, Virginia. When investors saw how Sprague's system allowed communities to expand, they quickly adopted it. By 1895, almost nine hundred trolley lines and nearly eleven thousand miles of track had been built in the United States.

By 1890, an electric railway was just what Pottstown needed, as the borough was in a period of explosive growth. In 1888, by annexing part of Lower Pottsgrove Township, the borough had spread out to the north and east, and its population had burgeoned from 5,305 to 13,696.

In reaction to this growth, Pottstown eventually had three trolley lines that would facilitate travel in town as well as connect it to other communities. First on the scene was the Pottstown Passenger Railway, which made its debut on June 15, 1893. The line's success led to the formation of the Ringing Rocks Electric Railway Company, which began operation on June 16, 1894. The third line arrived on May 28, 1908, when the cars of the Schuylkill Valley Traction Company began to service Pottstown.

The Pottstown Passenger Railway's course ran down the middle of High Street from the post office in Stowe into Lower Pottsgrove Township, where it turned south along Sanatoga Road to its eastern terminus at Sanatoga Park, a distance of slightly more than five miles.

The right of way was excavated by a combination of horsepower and pick and shovel. The *Daily Pottstown Ledger* reported that there was a "large force of men and about twelve big horses" at Stowe to begin the work on March 23. The excavation was done with a huge plow pulled by six horses that tore up the earth and cobblestones, while in its wake followed two scrappers,

A Pottstown trolley on its way to Sanatoga Park. *Courtesy of the Pottstown Historical Society.*

each pulled by two horses that cleared the loose dirt and piled it along the side of the ditch.

On June 10, 1893, the line was tested when a car packed with local dignitaries traveled from Stowe to High and Penn Streets in Pottstown. Throngs of people lined the road as the car pulled away "amid loud bangs, clangs, and wangs" from its "large gong."

The car cruised along West High Street amid the din of cheers and blasts from locomotives on the nearby railroad tracks, the noise startling passing horses and causing them to "career about and stand directly on their hind legs," while the "heavy director of the road," apparently carried away by all the excitement, "pulled off his hat and swung it round in exultation." When the line opened officially on June 15, the press to ride was so heavy that the company recorded 2,681 fares.

These first trolley cars were colorful and ornate. Their exteriors were cream yellow and maroon, with the company's name emblazoned in large gilt letters along both sides and the running gear painted rich reddish brown. The interiors were almost opulent, with Wilton-carpeted bench seats amid cherry wood and ceilings of black trimmed with bird's-eye maple.

Included in the company's $90,000 start-up costs were thirteen acres of land in Lower Pottsgrove Township along Sanatoga Road, where it created Sanatoga Park, a family amusement park with picnic tables, a dance pavilion, rides and a man-made lake. This complex was an instant

Two Pottstown trolley crewmen pose with their machine. *Courtesy of the Pottstown Historical Society.*

hit, drawing huge crowds that got there largely by buying fares on the company's trolleys.

In the wake of the Passenger Railway's success, it didn't take long for another group of Pottstown businessmen to copy the idea of a trolley line combined with an amusement park. The Ringing Rocks Railway Company bought two hundred acres of land north of Pottstown on Ringing Hill and developed it into Ringing Rocks Park.

The company's trolley line ran between the park and the Philadelphia and Reading Railroad station on South Hanover Street. Although it ran north–south, there were a few turns, so for a few blocks the tracks ran east–west to bridge the space between Hanover and Charlotte Streets. On the northern part of the route, the tracks turned east at present-day Mervine Street and crossed open fields before turning north again and crossing Sprogel's Run on a 180-foot-long trestle and climbing a steep hill to arrive at the park's pavilion. Years later, a Pottstown resident recalled the ascent as "a long steep climb up the hill from the power house at the bottom…and often the trolley slowed down its eight miles an hour pace to make [it]."

Because the company's line traveled a short distance through town, most of its income came from fares paid by people going to Ringing Rocks Park. This scenario drove the line out of business in October 1905, but it came back after that as the Boyertown to Pottstown Electric Railway Company, a subsidiary of the Schuylkill Valley Traction (SVT) Company.

Schuylkill Valley was in turn part of an ambitious plan to establish trolley service from Philadelphia to Harrisburg. To help achieve this goal, the Traction Company bought the Ringing Rocks Company in 1906, and by 1908, it had extended that line north to Swamp Pike at Romig Road. From there it ran along the pike into Boyertown, where passengers could board another trolley that would take them to Reading.

SVT brought its first trolley into Pottstown on May 28, 1908, making it possible to ride the SVT trolleys from Chestnut Hill all the way into Reading. SVT came into Pottstown on the east by running the line parallel and slightly north of High Street. After crossing Sprogel's Run near Sunny Brook, the line turned southwest, crossing High Street and turning west again to cross Moser Road, then going along Queen Street, only to turn north on Adams Street and finally following King Street west to Manatawny.

With tens of thousands of trips in cars that could cruise at thirty-five miles an hour, there were surprisingly few accidents. One fatality occurred on the Schuylkill Valley Transit line on July 31, 1913. That morning, the overhead electric trolley wire broke and fell on the roof of a car. The live wire produced "flashes of fire" and "switched around the car," creating panic among the passengers. One of them bailed out while the trolley was still moving and was killed when she fell and broke her neck. The most spectacular accident came on July 16, 1921, at the base of Rahn's Hill on High Street, just east of present-day Sunny Brook. A trolley coming down the hill lost its brakes and slammed head-on into another car just coming onto the mainline from a switch. The front of both cars was demolished, and the impact sent slivers of glass and showers of wooden splinters through the cars, killing three and injuring forty-three. One of the dead was the motorman of the eastbound car who was found pinned in the wreckage. One of his legs was torn off by the crash and the other, badly damaged, had to be amputated on-site to free him from his trolley.

For twenty-one years, the center of Pottstown was crisscrossed by a maze of trolley tracks as cars from the three lines ran up and down, back and forth and in and out of the borough. This scene began to change in 1927, when SVT discontinued its service between Boyertown and Pottstown. Five years later, it did the same between Pottstown and Collegeville.

That left the Pottstown Passenger Railway as Pottstown's last trolley line. However, it was soon forced to yield to the onslaught of the internal combustion engine as automobiles and buses, not bound to tracks, became America's preferred means of transportation.

Late in the evening on September 30, 1936, in a heavy rain, the last trolley run in Pottstown began. *Mercury* reporter J. Ernest Spare described how the "antiquated cars" passed over the "rough and broken jointed rails" while "a crowd of happy passengers" sang "The Old Grey Mare" accompanied by two young ladies playing an "air whistle and a foot gong." When the run finished, the trolleys were left sitting in the rain in what Spare felt was an "ignoble end."

The next morning, workers from Mayer Pollock began a rapid removal of all traces of the old Pottstown line; the tracks were ripped up and wires and poles torn down. As for the cars, some went on to become roadside produce stands or chicken coops, while the rest were scrapped.

POTTSTONIANS CELEBRATE PRESIDENTIAL ELECTIONS

Before World War II, Americans were much more active in politics than those of present vintage. The rallies and victory celebrations were not only social occasions, but also, in an era before civil service reform, the winning party had seemingly unlimited largess at its disposal to distribute to the ranks of the faithful.

Nineteenth-century Americans were not impressed with brevity and expected long speeches and sermons. Thus, everyone was thrilled when Pennsylvania's United States congressman and former Speaker of the House of Representatives Galusha A. Grow spoke for two hours at Pottstown's Opera House while campaigning for Republican candidate James Garfield in 1880.

As an aside, the Pennsylvania German dialect was still so widely spoken in the Pottstown area that at a Democratic rally in Sanatoga in 1892, the feature speaker delivered his talk in German.

As popular as the speeches were, thousands more attended the parades and rallies of these campaigns. By the 1880 presidential contest between Republican James A. Garfield and Democrat Winfield Scott Hancock, the campaign parades had reached their height of lavishness. On

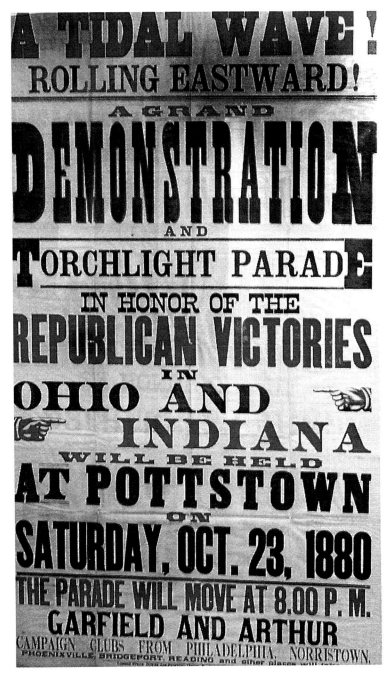

A James Garfield for president poster from Pottstown. *Courtesy of George Wausnock.*

October 25, the Republicans of West Chester staged a parade that had 10,000 men in line, followed the next night by a Republican parade in Norristown with 9,025 marchers and one at Phoenixville that drew an estimated 20,000 spectators.

On Saturday night, October 26, Pottstown's GOP lured over four thousand men into a "grand parade lighted with blazing torches." In an era before paving, the town's streets were vulnerable to bad weather, but even though it had rained Friday night and into Saturday morning, the "first three hundred men tramped the mud into a level floor and conditions were fine for marching."

The logistics involved in organizing the parade and transporting thousands of participants and spectators to Pottstown were daunting. (In 1880, the borough had 5,313 residents, which means that on that evening Pottstown's population more than doubled.) The railroad handled the transportation, running special trains from as far as Philadelphia and Reading. Pottstown ladies made twelve thousand sandwiches to feed the multitude, consuming in the process nine hundred loaves of bread, 215 pounds of butter and one hundred hams.

Light played a large role in these parades. Many houses were now equipped with gas, and their residents would turn on all their lights, illuminating homes and businesses from "cellar to attic"; they would intensify the effect by decorating with Chinese lanterns and candles. Fireworks of all kinds and colors also lit the sky, while every parade had several wagons in the line of march from which Roman candles, rockets and other potentially incendiary devices were fired as the procession moved through town.

Political clubs constituted the largest part of these parades. In 1860, the most popular were the Wide Awakes, a club started by young Republicans in Hartford, Connecticut, that rapidly spread throughout the North. The Wide Awakes—whose name was a pun on the fact that their caps were made from fabric that had no nap—wore a uniform that included a hat and cape, with each member carrying a fence rail (a reference to Abe Lincoln, the rail splitter) topped with a torch for nighttime parades. In October 1860, Pottstown Republicans hosted an all-day rally that five area Wide Awake clubs, totaling five hundred men, attended. During the parade, they were an awesome sight as their column, lit by five hundred torches, wended its way through the borough's streets, reminding one spectator of a "river of fire."

The political clubs grew in number from 1860 to 1880 so that, by the latter date, Pottstown alone boasted seven of these organizations, including

A large crowd greets Theodore Roosevelt at the Pottstown station during the 1912 presidential election. *Courtesy of the Pottstown Historical Society.*

"junior clubs" for teenage boys. For that year's presidential contest, Pottstown's Pioneer Corps of the Young Men's Superb Democratic Pioneer Club had new uniforms. There was a white shirt with a blue collar and cuffs, adorned on the front with a blue shield containing the letters "H.E. in Roman." The headgear was a zinc helmet with a copper spearhead on top and a web band of the same material. The ensemble was complemented with a "carry axe worked in imitation of metal, which was used for drilling."

On parade, the Pioneers performed intricate drills. The *Pottstown Ledger* noted that the Friendship Pioneer Club of Phoenixville was adept at "lighting and silent axe drill" and "fancy marching" that included "corners, triangles and hollow squares." Not to be outdone, the Pottstowners were seen on High Street one evening "drilling for close torchlight parade." The men became proficient enough that their performance in a Norristown exhibition was thought by a reporter from the *Philadelphia Record* to have been "especially notable."

The 1880 version of the Pottstown Pioneers looked snappy and marched well, but occasionally they got into trouble. On the night before the election, they attended a large rally in Boyertown. During its course, the *Pottstown Daily Ledger* noted that "there was considerable disturbance at the outskirts of the audience, with sundry persons shouting, 'Hurrah for Hancock!'" Despite the heckling, the program concluded without any trouble. However, as the "Pioneer Club of Pottstown fell into line to march to the depot," Alexander Sassaman from Gilbertsville, who "occasioned much of the previous disturbance, again cheered for Hancock and made sundry other demonstrations."

This final outburst was the flash point for "several members of the Pioneer Club," who "made a rush" for Sassaman. Alarmed at the sight of several men with hatchets advancing on him, Sassaman pulled out a pistol and fired. The shot grazed the finger of Samuel Fryer, one of the Pioneers, and then struck sixteen-year-old Edward Grimm of Boyertown in the hip and deflected downward, burying itself in his thigh. It was then that Sassaman was "terribly struck on the head by an axe [hatchet] in the hands of one of the Pioneer Club." The wounded Grimm and Sassaman were taken away for medical attention.

The next morning, an "attaché of the *Leader*" visited Sassaman at his home, where he found the much-damaged man. His eyes were swollen almost shut and his head was "considerably bruised," with a two-inch cut on its left side and "a more serious wound on the top of the cranium," where a piece of the outer skull had been chipped off, and there was a large gash, which had been sewn shut the night before. Both Sassaman and Grimm survived their injuries. The hatchet-wielder, who was Samuel Fryer, was later arrested by the Berks County sheriff and arraigned on a charge of assault with attempted murder. Bail was set at $2,000, a very large amount of money in 1880, which was posted by Henry Gabel, the owner of the Pottstown Roller Mill.

As the century progressed, the lavish campaign parades faded, while the victory celebrations became more frenetic. Following the election of 1916, the *Pottstown News* noted that "general apathy was in command during the campaign in this borough, but last night all the pent up energies of the inhabitants, old and young, seemed to break forth all at once."

There was always a tinge of the saturnalia in these events. As early as 1880, the *Pottstown Daily Ledger* groused about the post-election festivities on High Street, claiming that the combination of "considerable drunkenness" and "several fights" sounded like a "first-class riot."

Through the first decades of the twentieth century, it seems as if events were beginning to get out of hand. Both parties' headquarters were near the central intersection of High and Hanover Streets. From this point—via telegraph and, later, telephone lines—the latest election results would be posted on huge screens, providing people with the only way to follow the presidential race. Because of this, High Street became a magnet for thousands. Obviously, there was a legitimate interest in the election results, but with a milling crowd filling the streets and sidewalks, the atmosphere was sometimes rowdy.

Based on the reading of newspaper accounts, it is clear that Tuesday, November 11, 1908, must go down in history as the wildest election ever seen in Pottstown. According to the *Daily News*, a "large crowd" produced some "lively scenes," and it was obvious that the police had no control over events.

Bonfires, which had always been part of election evenings, were banned for the first time. But no official proclamation was going to stop this popular custom. A large fire built at the intersection of High and Hanover was "extinguished by the police," but another soon sprang to life "at a different spot," and the "police were powerless to do anything about it." In fact, the bonfires were fed all evening by "teams hauling supplies" to them. For hours, through the milling crowds, "a band of calathumpian order headed a procession of madly cheering men and boys up and down High Street to 'Hail Hail the Gang's All Here.'" In the meantime, the "paddle [from the context of the article, a flat piece of wood applied to the south side of a north-walking person]…made its appearance again and young women and girls joined the boys and men in making life miserable for the pedestrians." Over top of this whizzed skyrockets and Roman candles.

Wednesday morning saw the downtown area in shambles, littered with debris and the ashes of bonfires and awash in tons of confetti. There were probably more than a few hangovers and a scattering of black eyes. George Stout, the borough's truant officer, had a big day, visiting the homes of thirty-five high school students who were absent. Stout's visits were not always courteously received. One irate mother wished that "this country was ruled by a king, so she would not be bothered by his visit" and further vented by "threatening to throw a pot of scalding water on him if he didn't stay away from her home."

With the passing of time, these election-night celebrations morphed into decorous processions that featured a short parade with a few bands and a float or two, following which most people went home or had a few at a club or bar that stayed open despite the election-day ban. A century after the 1908 debacle, presidential campaign activity and victory celebrations were almost extinct at the local level. Television ruled the process, inundating citizens with an endless barrage of commercials, sound bites and programs for more than a year prior to the event; then, in many cases, by 11:00 p.m. on election day it predicted the winner to hundreds of millions while across the country the High Streets of America were dark and silent.

TWO POTTSTOWN FAMILIES AND THEIR HOMES

Gone and Forgotten

Pottstown moved from an idea in John Potts's mind to a reality 248 years ago, so by American standards it is an old community. Many families who played important roles in the town's early development have been forgotten. However, by poring over old history books and newspapers and wiping off years of accumulated dust on old photographs, it is possible to bring some of them and their times back to life. What follows are stories of two of these families.

For more than a century, a large stone house stood on the east side of Hanover Street just above South. Built by Jesse Ives in 1806, it was the home of his descendants for several generations. The son of William and Rebecca (Hockley) Ives, Jesse was born on March 5, 1771, in what was then New Hanover Township, Philadelphia County, but today is part of Pottstown. Records show that Ives was a successful businessman and a respected citizen in the town's earliest years. He was elected to the first borough council, appointed to the first board of directors of the Pottstown Library Company, elected to one term as burgess and was one of the trustees who oversaw the construction of the Hanover Street Bridge, the first bridge across the Schuylkill River.

From about 1800 to 1855, Ives owned and operated a gristmill on the west side of Hanover Street, north of present-day College Drive. The grounds had a mill on them from 1725 until 1977, and since 1985 they have been the location of the Roller Mill Apartments, created by rehabbing one of the mills, making it the oldest continuously occupied spot in the borough.

The Jesse Ives House, which once stood on South Hanover Street. *Courtesy of the Pottstown Historical Society.*

The mill was powered by water from a millrace that came from Manatawny Creek and emptied into the Schuylkill River just west of the present-day Hanover Street Bridge. After the Philadelphia and Reading Railroad began running through Pottstown, Ives leased the water rights of the race to the company in return for a permanent pass giving him the right to "pass in the passenger cars, over the railroad…whenever he may desire."

Jesses Ives died on November 28, 1860. In his obituary, Pottstown's newspaper noted not only his "vigorous intellect and retentive memory" but also that he "lived and died a humble and consistent member of the Society of Friends." He is buried at the Potts Burial Ground on Chestnut Street.

At some point, Jesse Ives's daughter, Mary Ann; her husband, Charles P. Rutter; and their children moved in with him. The branches of Rutter's family tree were so tightly intertwined that three of his grandparents were Potts and the other (obviously) a Rutter. He was a direct descendant of Thomas Potts and Thomas Rutter, the two men who pioneered the iron industry in this area, and also of John Potts, the founder of Pottstown.

Given his background, it comes as no surprise to learn that Rutter started out as an iron maker; however, he later worked for the Philadelphia and

Reading Railroad, which probably explains why he came to live in Pottstown instead of Pine Forge.

Rutter, his father-in-law and a few others in the area were active abolitionists for many years prior to the Civil War. Even in the northern states, where slavery was illegal, these people were by and large very unpopular and, as an abolitionist from Norristown later wrote, "brought upon ourselves the blackguardism of the vulgar and the stern opposition of the so-called respectable people."

Rutter and Ives were involved in the Underground Railroad, a very loosely organized network of people who provided shelter and aid to runaway slaves. When the United States Congress passed the Fugitive Slave Act of 1850 making it illegal to aid runaways, this activity became very risky. According to one of Rutter's daughters, their family and others in the area "sheltered and concealed" fugitive slaves in their "barns, outhouses, and kitchens, and when the opportunity came they were sent further on at night by an old colored man who was himself a runaway slave." It isn't known for certain, but it's very likely that the Ives/Rutter family also hid fugitives in the mill.

After Ives's death, the Rutters continued to live in the house he built. Charles Rutter died there two days after Christmas 1887, after being "sick and afflicted some two years or more by mental and body infirmities." On the last day of the year, he was buried at Edgewood Cemetery on High and Keim Streets.

Charles Rutter opened his home to his son-in-law and his family just as Jesse Ives had done for him. In 1865, his daughter Mary Elizabeth married William M. Hobart. Born in Pottstown in 1841, Hobart knew the Rutter family well; he had served in the Union army during the Civil War with Mary's brother Sam. Not surprisingly, he became involved in the iron business but later was a mining engineer. In 1918, Mary Elizabeth Hobart died, and with the children gone, William, now seventy-seven years old, moved in with his daughter, who lived only four blocks away. He died there in 1924 and, like the rest of his family, was buried at Edgewood Cemetery.

After Hobart's departure, the house stood empty for four years. With this part of Pottstown now almost totally commercial and industrial, the property was ripe for development. In October 1922, the *Pottstown News* announced that the "Old Rutter Homestead" had been purchased by the Aurora Knitting Mills. That company razed the house and built a factory there but never used it. A year later, Robert Feroe bought it for

Jacob S. Yost. *From* A History of Montgomery County Illustrated, *1884.*

his paper box manufacturing business. Eventually, Mrs. Smith's Pies, one of Pottstown's largest employers, became the owner, pulverized it and built a modern plant on the site. Today, Mrs. Smith's Pies is gone and so is its factory.

About thirty years after Jesse Ives built his house on Hanover Street, Jacob S. Yost, a member of the United States Congress, built a mansion on the southwest corner of High and Charlotte Streets. The son of John Y. and Anna Maria (Senewell) Yost, Jacob was born on July 29, 1801, on the family farm in what is now Lower Pottsgrove Township. In 1820, Yost enrolled in an academy in Philadelphia where he studied mathematics

The Yost mansion at the southwest corner of High and Charlotte Streets. *Courtesy of the Pottstown Historical Society.*

and surveying. After that, he returned to work on the family farm, but in 1826, he traded in the plow for a printer's apron when he bought a half interest in the *Lafayette Aurora*, a weekly newspaper published in Pottstown. That same year, the young publisher married Anna M. Childe of Pottstown. Over the next decade, the couple had four children, but Anna died sometime around 1835.

Yost also had an affinity for politics, where his "intelligence and activity" combined with his "kindly disposition and genial manners" earned him a seat in the Pennsylvania House of Representatives from 1836 to 1839. Four years later, he was elected to the United States House of Representatives and served there until 1847.

After he left Congress, Yost returned to Pottstown. In 1857, President James Buchanan named Yost the United States marshal for the eastern district of Pennsylvania, a post that he held until 1860. Jacob Yost died in Pottstown on March 7, 1872, and was buried at Edgewood Cemetery.

George Yost Coffin, a nephew of Jacob Yost and a well-known political cartoonist and illustrator. *Courtesy of Special Collections and University Archives, Gelman Library, George Washington University.*

While he was in the nation's capital, Yost met Miss Mary A. Harrington, "one of the belles of the city," who was known for her brilliance, "marked conversational ability and intimate knowledge of Washington statesmanship." She swept him off his feet, and they were married in Washington on December 26, 1844. Yost brought his wife back to Pottstown and built for her a fine mansion at the southwest corner of High and Charlotte Streets.

Mary Yost was a devout Presbyterian, and presumably for her sake, Yost also became one. When they moved to the borough, Pottstown didn't have a Presbyterian church, so he set about founding one. By 1849, the town had its first Presbyterian congregation.

Mary Yost's sister, Sarah Harrington Coffin, soon joined her in Pottstown, and in March 1850, Sarah's son George Yost Coffin was born in the Yost home. George Y. Coffin went on to become one of America's best-known political cartoonists during the 1880s and '90s. In addition to being the *Washington Post*'s first cartoonist, his work also appeared in *Harper's Illustrated*, *Puck*, the *Evening Star*, the *Critic*, the *Sunday Herald* and the *National Tribune*.

Even though the Coffins moved to Washington, D.C., in 1855, the two small families remained very close, and Sarah and George came to Pottstown often. In fact, Sarah Coffin died at the Yost home on March 4, 1891, and is buried in their lot at Edgewood Cemetery. When George Coffin died in Washington on November 28, 1896, his body was also buried at Edgewood. Mary Yost, who was the last to go, died at her home on June 13, 1900, and two days later, she joined the rest of the family at Edgewood.

Less than a year after the death of its mistress, the Yost mansion was demolished, and by 1904, two new buildings occupied the Yost property. At the rear was a market house, and at the front, which bordered on High Street, was the auditorium building, an impressive three-story structure of red and white sandstone with a corner tower 106 feet high.

In 1922, Robert Feroe, who also owned the box company factory on the Ives site, bought the auditorium building and turned the street-level portion into a shopping arcade. As that project neared completion, the *Pottstown News* opined that Feroe's creation "equals and in many respects rivals the Arcades which are so successfully being operated in all large cities" and enthused that because of it and other recent changes on High Street, the borough's "business section…can now be classed with other up-to-the-minute live-wire towns."

Two years later, Feroe sold the building to Harry J. Bahr, and thus it became known for the rest of its existence as the Bahr Arcade. In 1973, a little more than fifty years after its creation, the Bahr Arcade was torn down, and the ground became the Bahr Parking Lot.

FROM THE SANDLOTS TO THE MAJOR LEAGUES

Pottstown Plays the National Game

In the last half of the nineteenth century, America's burgeoning love affair with baseball—fueled in large part by the rising popularity of the professional game—elevated the sport to the status of a cultural icon that provided all classes of American society with a common bond. Baseball was not only the provenance of young boys on a lazy summer afternoon, but it was also played by millions of adults in every setting, from organized leagues to ad hoc games at church picnics or family reunions. A random sampling of Pottstown newspapers from the late 1860s to the 1950s reveals that Pottstown, in its enthusiasm for baseball, was a perfect microcosm of this national phenomenon.

The earliest record of Pottstown men playing baseball is found in a September 1861 letter of a Civil War soldier who mentioned that the "baseball club of our company [Company A, Fifty-third Pennsylvania] played [a] very exciting game [that] lasted more than four hours, and resulted in the complete victory of the Pottstown boys."

In the years immediately following the war, it was obvious that baseball was taking hold in Pottstown as the *Pottstown Ledger* wrote almost daily about the Seminole and Madison baseball clubs and a few with tongue-in-cheek names like the Waltzing Elephants and the Rattlesnakes. The paper reported on September 4, 1874, that the reptiles "had a hitch at the national game" against the Reading Modocs, powered by "Shacknasty Jim," who "used their war clubs with such effect"—they beat Pottstown 52–26—that the Rattlesnakes "had to crawl in their holes."

Through the late 1880s until America's entry into World War I in 1918, there was usually a semipro team from Pottstown that competed with

An 1890s Pottstown baseball team.

clubs from the surrounding area. From 1883 to 1893, the Pottstown Alerts occupied that niche. On September 9, 1891, seven hundred people paid ten cents apiece for men and fifteen cents for women to watch the Alerts beat the Philadelphia Athletics 1–0 in an exhibition game on the Pottstown ball field at Third and Manatawny Streets. Up until World War II, these games featuring professional teams against the local semipros were common. (Older Pottstown residents remember the Phillies playing games at the field in South Pottstown in the 1930s.) The A's owner was chronically short of cash, so a guaranteed purse made him amenable.

Pottstown team members were also paid. The *Ledger* mentioned in September 1891 that the Alerts star player had been enticed by an offer of forty-five dollars to play with Reading for the rest of the month. Money was always scarce, which is why Alerts player-manager Harry Shinehouse "leased the land across the Manatawny [Creek] over where the ice house stands and the land to the north and south of the grounds" to prevent "snide game viewers" from watching for free.

Pottstown's Industrial League came on the baseball scene in the 1930s. As the name implies, it was made up of teams from the town's many factories and steel plants, like Spicer's or Bethlehem Steel, although there were also teams sponsored by other groups such as the Am Vets and, in later years, Bechtel's Sport Shop. Most of their games were played at Franklin Field, located behind what is today the Pottstown Middle School on North Franklin Street. There were many excellent players in the league, and over the years, some of them were in Major League farm systems. Douglas Schaeffer tried out with the St. Louis Cardinals, and Clyde Umstead, an imposing leftie, had a run with the Chicago White Sox.

During the 1950s, the Pottstown High School varsity baseball team, the Trojans, dominated high school ball in the Pottstown area. Between April 19, 1951, and May 11, 1954, the Trojans won forty-eight straight games, thus establishing a national record for consecutive wins by a high school baseball team.

Pottstown residents quickly donated $1,500 to send the players and coaches to an induction ceremony at the Baseball Hall of Fame in Cooperstown, New York. Early on Saturday morning, June 19, in a motorcade with police escort, the group traveled to the airport at Reading and boarded a charter that flew to Utica, New York. From there, it was a forty-mile bus ride to Cooperstown. It was an unforgettable experience, so it is easy to understand why, forty-nine years later, Carl Sundstrom, a team member, exclaimed, "I can say to my grandchildren 'Hey! Your grandfather's name is in the Baseball Hall of Fame Museum,' and I'm sure that all of the guys are also that proud."

Because of the strong local baseball culture, it comes as no surprise that at least six Pottstown men, including two pairs of brothers, played in the Major Leagues. George Daniel Weaver Jr., better known as "Buck," was born in Pottstown on August 18, 1890, and grew up in Stowe. From 1912 through 1920, he played third base and shortstop for the Chicago White Sox, then one of baseball's strongest teams. Weaver's career statistics are impressive. His lifetime batting average was .272, but for his last three years of play, he averaged .309; in his final season, he hit .324. Weaver also excelled in the field, especially at third base. The ultimate tribute to his play there came from the great Ty Cobb, who lamented the futility of trying to bunt against Buck: "I'd see that filthy uniform standing there, that funny face grinning at me, and I wanted to lay one down that line more than anything in the world. The s.o.b. throwed me out every time."

Weaver appeared in two World Series: in 1917, he hit .333 as the White Sox won the world championship by defeating the New York Giants, and in 1919, he hit .324 and played errorless ball in the White Sox loss to the Cincinnati Reds.

Buck Weaver as a member of the Chicago White Sox. *Courtesy of ClearBuck.com.*

It was the 1919 series that ended Weaver's career. In 1920, he and seven of his teammates, as well as two professional gamblers, were charged with conspiring to throw the Series. (Weaver was present when the fix was discussed but never took a dime of the money.) The players were tried and found not guilty, but in 1921, Judge Kennesaw Mountain Landis, baseball's first commissioner, suspended them from baseball for life. Over the years, Danny Weaver made several unsuccessful attempts to get reinstated into the game. After his death in Chicago on January 31, 1956, his two nieces unsuccessfully took up his cause, and now there are several websites, including ClearBuck. com, devoted to him and lobbying for his reinstatement.

Bobby (Robert Clayton) Shantz was born in Pottstown on September 26, 1925. A right-handed pitcher, Schantz played sixteen seasons in the Majors, winning 199 games and losing 99. He made his first appearance with the Philadelphia Athletics in 1949 and his last in 1964 with the Philadelphia Phillies. During his career, Shantz was named to the American League All-Star Team three times, won eight Golden Gloves and appeared in the 1957 and 1960 World Series with the New York Yankees. His best year was 1952, when the five-foot, six-and-a-half-inch right-hander won 24 games for the Philadelphia Athletics—31 percent of the team's victories that season—and earned the American League's Most Valuable Player award.

Billy (Wilmer Ebert) Shantz, Bobby's younger brother, was born in Pottstown on July 31, 1927. He played two full seasons: 1954 with the Philadelphia Athletics and 1955 with the A's when they moved to Kansas City. Following a four-year absence from the game, the New York Yankees bought his contract in 1959, and his career ended in 1960 after appearing in one game with that team.

Dick Ricketts Jr., born in Pottstown on December 4, 1933, played professional basketball and baseball. He was the first-round draft pick of the St. Louis Hawks in 1955 and spent three seasons in the NBA. That same year, the St. Louis Cardinals signed him as a free agent, and after he left pro basketball, he had a one-year career pitching in twelve games with the Cards in 1959.

His brother, Dave Ricketts, born in Pottstown on July 12, 1935, was a catcher with the St. Louis Cardinals in 1963 and from 1965 through 1969. His last year as a player was 1970 with the Pittsburgh Pirates. In 1967 and '68, he was in the World Series with the Cardinals, making him the third Pottstown native to play in the Fall Classic.

Howie Bedell, a native of Clearfield, Pennsylvania, came to Pottstown as a child in 1944. In 1957, Bedell entered the Milwaukee Braves farm system. Five years later, he opened the 1962 season as the Braves' left fielder, and the *Sporting News* named him and "Boog" Powell (Baltimore Orioles first baseman) as "prize rookies." Bedell was out of professional ball before that season ended, but in 1968, the Philadelphia Phillies called him up for a cup of coffee. In a game against the Los Angeles Dodgers, he hit a run-scoring sacrifice fly that ended Hall of Fame pitcher Don Drysdale's record of consecutive shutout innings.

Part III

POTTSTOWN MOVES INTO THE TWENTIETH CENTURY

From Sleepy Village to Boomtown

WHAT THEY DID FOR FUN

Life in Pottstown a Century Ago

One hundred years ago, Pottstown was a prosperous and growing community with electricity, running water, public transportation, telephones and many of the other amenities associated with modern urban society. The town's residents worked in steel plants, ironworks, boiler factories, textile mills, stores and offices, and sprinkled into that mix was a large number of professional people such as doctors, dentists, engineers and attorneys.

No matter their occupation, Pottstowners worked long hours, with ten- and twelve-hour days being common. In April 1907, Pottstown's barbers complained because they had to stay open on Saturdays until midnight; they claimed that there was no business after 11:00 p.m. That summer, many of the merchants announced that they were curtailing their hours and closing their stores at 8:00 p.m. on weekdays and 10:00 p.m. on Fridays and Saturdays, but doctors and dentists maintained their evening and Saturday office hours.

Pottstown's Grand Opera House ended its life as the Victor Movie Theatre and was torn down in the 1950s. *Courtesy of the Pottstown Historical Society.*

Pottstown also offered many ways for its residents to spend what free time they had. For anyone who wanted to just sit back and be entertained, Pottstown had theatres and movie houses. Pottstown's connection to two railroads, its position between Reading and Philadelphia and its proximity to New York City made it an ideal stop for traveling theatre companies and vaudeville acts, providing local folks with live performances several nights a week.

Pottstown Moves into the Twentieth Century

The Grand Opera House, which began its existence as a market house, was Pottstown's largest theatre and therefore the site of the most elaborate shows. On Monday, November 11, 1907, a new production of *Uncle Tom's Cabin*, based on the Harriet Beecher Stowe novel of 1851, opened there. According to an ad in the *Ledger*, this "scenic and electrical display" was the "grandest" production of this perennial favorite "ever executed." It featured "fifty actors, a carload of special scenery, a solo orchestra of ten musicians, singers and dancers, and ten Russian and Cuban Bloodhounds," which were billed as the "most dangerous, man-eating blood hounds ever seen."

In addition to the Grand Opera House, there were several smaller theatres in town that booked one- and two-person vaudeville acts. Some of them sound quaint today, such as *Pete La Mar, America's Greatest Yodeler*, but Pottstonians did have the opportunity to see some very talented professionals whose careers were on the way up. One example was Harry Carey Sr., who became a big star in silent movie westerns, making fourteen of them with the famous film director John Ford. Carey was also the actor John Wayne copied in his early film career.

The small theatres also showed movies. These were the days of the nickelodeons, when storage rooms and storefronts were converted into theatres that showed movies for a nickel. Pottstown had many of these in the early 1900s, among them the Gem, the Princess (a large storeroom in the Auditorium Building), the Star, the Acme and the Savoy.

An ad in the April 12, 1909 edition of the *Ledger* noted that the Gem Moving Picture Parlor, now under new management, was showing three reels and an illustrated song. The ad also claimed that the Gem was "the most conservative picture house in town," underscoring the fact that according to one movie historian, these one-reel movies often had "immoral subject matter."

The illustrated song, very popular at the time, was a song with the words shown on the screen in a series of hand-painted colored slides. Occasionally, the theatre manager hired a vocalist to sing it, but often the audience belted out the tune accompanied by the theatre's pianist.

Music and sports were very popular in town. In 1907, the only way to enjoy music was through live performances or playing it oneself, and according to the newspapers, Pottstown citizens did both. Because of the do-it-yourself nature of music, many homes had a piano in the front parlor, and families sang, not just in unison but also harmonies.

Playing the piano and singing in the home were so popular that thousands of newspapers, including the *Daily Ledger*, published a weekly song with

The Auditorium Building, built in 1905 and later known as the Bahr Arcade, was the site of Pottstown's first movie theatre. *Courtesy of the Pottstown Historical Society.*

piano accompaniment. These were popular tunes of the day, and works by the Shubert Brothers and even George M. Cohan appeared. On July 17, 1909, the selection was "Come Over on My Veranda," a waltz with music by Lester W. Keith and lyrics by John Kemble, as "sung by Julian Eltinge, America's Leading Sex Simulator." Eltinge, whose real name was William Julian Dalton, was a very famous onstage female impersonator in vaudeville and, later, silent movies. At the time, most Pottstown residents would have recognized his name.

In addition to the scores of ladies who gave private piano and voice lessons, Edna Valeria Boyer and Alfred W. Weiser had music schools in Pottstown, and their students gave frequent public recitals. In 1909, Weiser, who lived at 158 North Hanover Street, was completing his twenty-first year as the organist at Emmanuel Lutheran Church, while Boyer, who lived with her parents at 248 Beech Street, was just beginning as a piano teacher.

Pottstown citizens who dabbled in instrumental music had their choice of several community bands and orchestras to play in. In 1907, the

The Pottstown High School Alumni Orchestra on the Grand Opera House stage. *Courtesy of the Pottstown Historical Society.*

Pottstown High School Alumni Association formed an orchestra, which prospered over the years. Its first rehearsal was at the home of Henry Sotter on York Street, and by 1909, the group had advanced to the point where it was doing a series of subscription concerts at the Grand Opera House. The group's pianist was Miss Lotta Young, who is still remembered by many Pottstownites.

Without a doubt, the town's premier musical organization was the Pottstown Band. Directed by Hugh J. High, a forty-eight-year-old farmer and cornet player who lived in North Coventry Township, the band rehearsed in a room above Weitzenkorn's store on High Street. In 1907, High brought the famous cornet soloist Herbert L. Clarke to Pottstown to perform with the band. (Clarke at the time was one of the country's most famous musicians, and over the years many Pottstown residents had heard him perform as a soloist with Sousa's Band and with his own band at Willow Grove Park.)

As in all American towns, sports were very popular in Pottstown. Of course, everybody—including women—played baseball in those days.

However, football and basketball were also beginning to catch on in the area. Pottstown High School (PHS) had fielded a football team since the 1890s. The Thanksgiving Day game tradition began in 1906, and in 1909, Pottstown High took the train to Phoenixville to play the "iron town's high school eleven." A large crowd of local fans and the Phillies Fire Company's fife and drum corps took a special train to Phoenixville to root for Pottstowners. (Today, when everyone is worried about America's youth being overweight, it is interesting to note that the average weight of the PHS team members was 133 pounds.)

Pottstown also had a few athletic clubs that fielded football and basketball teams. In 1906, Lloyd Leh, who managed a football team with the tongue-in-cheek name Schwoyer's Chair Warmers, had the unique idea of playing a game with the high school squad under the light of the moon. Unfortunately, the game never took place.

One of the most interesting concepts to come into play in this era was the idea of forming associations designed to improve people physically, mentally and morally. The Young Men's Christian Association is a perfect example of this philosophy. Founded by George Williams in London, England, in 1844, the organization eventually crossed the Atlantic, and the first YMCA in the United States opened in Boston in 1851.

The drive to bring a YMCA to Pottstown was spearheaded by John Meigs, owner and headmaster of the Hill School. Located in several floors of what is now Lastick's Furniture on the northwest corner of High and Charlotte Streets, the YMCA opened its doors in late January 1904. The quarters were equipped with a gymnasium, reading rooms and even a bowling alley, and a professional manager was hired as its director.

The YMCA almost immediately became a positive force in Pottstown. It bought land east of High and Keim Streets for athletic fields and sponsored many activities, from sports teams to current event discussions and Bible study groups. For several years, the YMCA sponsored men's meetings on Sunday afternoons at the Opera House. Only an hour long, these gatherings brought inspiring speakers from all over the United States, including John Raleigh Mott, who won a Nobel Peace Prize in 1946.

By the beginning of the twentieth century, Americans had become great club people. During the last quarter of the nineteenth century, secret fraternal organizations mushroomed in this country, and Pottstown, a microcosm of American society, was awash with them.

Two of the older societies, the Masons and the Odd Fellows, and two of the newer ones, the Elks and the Eagles, are familiar to us today. However, the number of these clubs and societies in Pottstown during the first decade of the twentieth century was so great as to require several articles to cover all of them. The Improved Order of Heptasophs (the seven wise men), the Imperial Order of Red Men, the Knights of the Ancient Order of the Mystic Chain, the Knights of the Golden Eagle, the Knights of Pythias, the Order of Independent Americans, the Patriotic Order of the Sons of America and the Royal Arcanum are a few of the lodges that met regularly (at least once a week) in Pottstown.

A LETHAL LOVE TRIANGLE LEAVES A POTTSTOWN MAN HANGING

"Day and Night I Was Pursued by This Woman"

On Monday, February 17, 1908, two Pottstown residents decided to go fishing in the Schuylkill River. As the men walked along the bank just above the mouth of Sprogel's Run, they spotted a coat floating in the water a few feet from shore. A closer look also revealed the backs of a pair of shoes. A few pokes with a fishing rod revealed that the shoes and coat were worn by a corpse.

The corpse was the body of a medium-sized man with sandy-colored hair and a moustache. An investigation soon revealed that it was the body of Michael Bodis of 454½ South Street, Pottstown, and that he died from a gunshot wound to the head. Stephen Sabo, a boarder in the Bodis home, quickly became the chief suspect, and the victim's wife, Elisabeth Bodis, was suspected as an accomplice.

Mike Bodis was born in 1872 near Budapest, Hungary. Bodis came to the United States in 1905, and a year later he was joined by his wife, Elisabeth Siga, their two children and Elisabeth's parents.

Sabo arrived in Pottstown from Hungary in 1907, leaving behind a wife and four children. In his mid-thirties, Sabo was the epitome of tall, dark and handsome, standing at six feet and weighing 165 pounds; he was considered, according to the *Daily News* of Pottstown, to have a "magnificent physique."

No photograph of Elisabeth Bodis has survived, but the *Daily News* described the fair-haired young mother as the "belle of the Hungarian colony," whose "striking appearance attracted much attention."

The months following Sabo's arrival at the Bodis home were tense. On September 1, Elisabeth gave birth to the couple's fourth child, Michael, who died a month later. The birth was difficult, and Elisabeth, faced with the loss of the baby plus the strain of caring for her three children and running a boardinghouse, was struggling. Lack of money was also a problem, so there was little cash to buy food. Neighbors later testified that Elisabeth could often be heard berating her husband. In January, Mike Bodis spent three weeks in Philadelphia looking unsuccessfully for work, but affairs in the Bodis home were no smoother after he returned.

Stephen Sabo worked very little after he moved in with the Bodis family and spent a lot of time around the house helping Elisabeth with the chores. It was also discovered that he occasionally bought her gifts and once took her to a show at the Phoenixville Opera House. Later, a local grocer testified that when the couple frequented his store, Sabo referred to Elisabeth as "my Mrs." and she called him "my Man."

In January, Sabo bought a pistol and ammunition at Fegley's hardware store in Pottstown. On Saturday, February 15, Sabo and Mike Bodis left home together. That afternoon, they did some work at the Campbell farm in Lower Pottsgrove Township and were last seen about 5:30 p.m. walking upstream toward the spot where the Pennsylvania Railroad Bridge crosses the Schuylkill River. At some point just above the mouth of Sprogel's Run, Sabo shot Mike Bodis once in the back of the head and threw his body in the river. With the high water and strong current, the murderer thought that the body would be carried downstream; instead, it washed into an eddy.

The body was identified the day it was found, and after the autopsy, Stephen Sabo was arrested. On February 22, at an inquest held in Pottstown, Sabo was indicted for murder, and Elisabeth Bodis was "censored" for her conduct. At a second hearing four days later, Sabo confessed that he murdered Bodis. He also claimed that for weeks Elisabeth Bodis had urged him to kill her husband so they could be together and that she had planned the killing and given him the money to buy the murder weapon. That evening, Elisabeth Bodis was arrested at her father's home and taken to Montgomery County Prison in Norristown on the 9:00 p.m. train.

The old Montgomery County Prison in Norristown where Stephen Sabo was executed. *Courtesy of the* Pottstown Mercury.

Stephan Sabo's trial began on June 4, 1908. On June 6 it took the jury less than three hours to find him guilty of murder, and he was sentenced to be hanged. Elisabeth Bodis's trial began on June 9. She was charged with "being an accessory before and after the fact of the willful and premeditated murder of her husband."

The evidence that she had an affair with Sabo was very strong, the most damning testimony coming from Justin Waraday, the other boarder at the Bodis home, who claimed that "Sabo and Mrs. Bodis were loving to each other" and that they "lived together as man and wife when Mr. Bodis was away." However, the only evidence that linked her to her husband's murder was Sabo's testimony, and the jury, feeling that this was not sufficient, found her not guilty the following day.

But Elisabeth Bodis wasn't going to escape that easily. Before she left the courthouse, she was arrested on a charge of adultery and sent back to jail. Tried and found guilty in October 1908, she was sentenced to a year in prison but was released for good behavior the following April after having spent 403 days behind bars. Upon her release, she was taken to her

The prison cell where Sabo spent his last night. *Courtesy of the* Pottstown Mercury.

father's home in Stowe, and that is the last mention of her in Pottstown-area records.

Stephan Sabo was hanged in Montgomery County Prison on July 29, 1909. As he stood on the platform gazing down at the large crowd of spectators, his final statement was read aloud. In it, he placed the responsibility for the murder on Elisabeth Bodis: "I had to do this deed. I had no rest. Day and night I was pursued by this woman."

To save his body from becoming the "subject of a medical school anatomy class," members of the Hungarian community raised thirty-seven dollars for his funeral expenses, which was enough to get him buried at Pottstown's Edgewood Cemetery. He was laid to rest only one plot away from the grave of Michael Bodis, the man he murdered.

POTTSTOWN MAN SHOOTS HIS WIFE

Gets Shocking Experience

On Saturday night, August 16, 1913, John Talap and his wife, Mary, of Howard Street in Stowe decided to leave their children with her parents and spend the evening in downtown Pottstown. It would just be the two of them. They would do some shopping, get something to eat, maybe take in a movie and then ride the trolley back home. It seemed like a wonderful way for a married couple to step out of their daily routine and spend a few hours together.

Their first stop was Leonard Gussman's store at 261 High Street, where John bought a coat and vest. The couple then walked two blocks east to Samuel Feurman's jewelry store; here, Mary waited outside while John bought a .32-caliber revolver and loaded it. Following this, John had a beer at Fryer's Saloon at 265 High Street, while Mary walked across the street for ice cream at Schwab's Ice Cream Parlor at 268 High. After this, they bought some fruit, went to a movie (probably at the Colonial at 249 High) and then took the trolley back to Stowe, where they got off at Rutter's Store at the intersection of High and Quinter and began walking toward their home.

It was raining, so Mary stopped at her parents' house to get an umbrella and a lantern. The couple walked to Race Street, where they took the dirt path across an open parcel of ground that led to their home. About fifty feet along the path, John Talap, walking on Mary's right, fell behind a step or two and then shot his wife twice with the revolver he had just bought at Feurman's store.

One bullet hit her right arm; the other smashed directly through the back of her neck and pulverized her second cervical vertebrae. Killed instantly, she fell over without a cry. The police found her body six hours later, her face lying in the mud, her purse in her left hand, the lantern in her right hand and the bullet that killed her in her mouth on the tip of her tongue.

John Talap fled. Although he had little money and spoke little English, he remained at large in southeastern Pennsylvania until the morning of August 21, when he burst into the office of an attorney in Norristown and exclaimed, "I am Talap; I shot and killed my wife!" The police were called, and they whisked Talap off on the train to Pottstown, where the next morning he was

A wanted poster for John Talap. *Courtesy of George Wausnock.*

arraigned on a charge of first-degree murder. He was then brought back to Norristown and placed in Montgomery County Prison to await his trial.

Born in Pennsylvania in 1890, Mary was the daughter of George and Mary Fesco. The Fescos were a large and close-knit family, and Mary, who was described by the *Pottstown Daily Ledger* as "comely and attractive," had an outgoing personality that made it easy for her to make friends.

By contrast, John Talap, who was born in Hungary in 1882 and came to America alone in 1903, was a taciturn and often sullen man with a suspicious nature and a bad temper. He could neither read nor write and spoke very broken English; however, at five feet, ten inches tall and a muscular 180 pounds, he had the strength to do the hard manual labor that was the lot of most immigrants at that time.

The couple was married in Reading, Pennsylvania, in 1906. The Talaps and their four children came to Stowe on April 1, 1913, along with Mary's parents and her brother and sister. Soon after their arrival, Talap got a job at Davidheiser's brickyard on Grosstown Road. He and his father-in-law bought three building lots on the north side of Vine Street, beginning at the intersection with School Lane, and hired a contractor to build houses on them. Until the homes were finished, the Talaps moved into No. 1 Schwartz's Row, on the north side of Howard Street, just west of Walnut, and the Fescos rented a home in Harnley's Row on the north side of Vine Street, just east of Quinter.

John Talap's trial began on October 10. Trial testimony painted a dark picture of the accusations and abuse that Mary Talap suffered at the hands of her husband. Anna Fesco, Mary's sister, stated that Mary "had been afraid of her husband for some time." In fact, her husband's behavior was so bizarre that once, before they moved to Stowe, he tied her to a pole, "pointed a revolver at her and threatened to kill her" because he believed that she was "too intimate with other men." Her brother, George, testified that after the birth of the couple's last child, Talap accused a Reading man of being the father. When he took this accusation to a justice of the peace, it was dismissed, and the accused quickly sued Talap for slander. In light of this litany of abuse, violence and suspicion, it is little wonder that Mary Talap's mother told the court that she was so concerned for her daughter's safety that, after they moved to Stowe, every evening she would peer in a window of the Talap house to make sure that Mary had not been harmed.

The trial took less than three full days. The state's case was very strong. The facts that Talap had abused his wife throughout their marriage, had threatened to kill her and had bought and loaded the murder weapon two hours before the shooting were damning points.

Talap's defense was ludicrous. He told the jury that his wife was shot when his revolver accidentally discharged when he slipped on the muddy path while transferring it from his right to left jacket pocket. At the trial, four people who lived near the murder site testified that they heard three shots that evening. In effect, Talap was asking the jury to believe that the

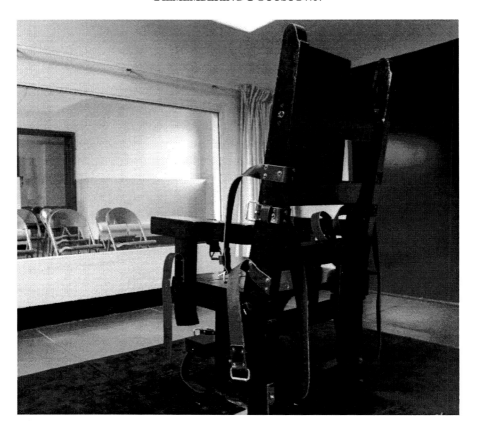

The electric chair in which John Talap was executed. *Courtesy of the Pennsylvania State Department of Corrections.*

weapon had accidentally fired three times and that two of those shots struck his wife. Talap also testified that he ran away after his wife screamed and fell over because he feared being beaten. In light of this, it is little wonder that the jury believed the prosecutor's assertion that Talap had lured his wife to Pottstown that night with the plan to kill her. It took the jury less than two hours to find him guilty of first-degree murder.

Ten days later, after a petition for a new trial was denied, Judge Aaron Schwartz sentenced Talap to death. The condemned man remained in Montgomery County Prison until February 9, 1915, when he was taken to Rockview Penitentiary near Bellefonte to await execution by electrocution.

Pennsylvania adopted electrocution as its official method of execution in May 1913, and John Talap was the first man in the commonwealth to be sentenced to die in that manner. Pennsylvania's electric chair and all of the auxiliary equipment were housed in a special block of rooms at Rockview Penitentiary.

The execution chamber was a concrete room, twenty-six by twenty-nine feet, with a small concrete shelf around three of its walls that served as seating for the witnesses. The chair, which reminded one witness of an "old English Morris Chair," occupied the center of the chamber. Attached to it were wide leather straps that would hold Talap's legs, elbows, wrists, chest and abdomen. Finally, there was a leather mask strapped to the chair to keep his head rigid. Suspended over the chair was "a powerful fan to draw off the smoke and possibly the smell of burning flesh."

At 7:00 a.m. on Tuesday, February 23, the witnesses were brought into the execution chamber. As soon as they were seated, a door opened quietly, and a Greek Catholic priest entered, followed by John Talap with a guard holding each of his arms. Talap was wearing a rough gray shirt and coarse trousers, the left leg flapping because of the long slit. His feet were clad in felt slippers and made no sound as he crossed the floor. After Talap entered, he

Mary Fesco's tombstone in St. John's Greek Catholic Church Cemetery on North Hanover Street in Pottstown. *Courtesy of the Pottstown Mercury.*

didn't look at any of the witnesses but stared only at the chair. As the guards strapped him in, the priest knelt in front of him praying.

When Talap was secured, the guards stepped back, and a white handkerchief was dropped. At that signal, an electrical engineer brought from Philadelphia turned a rheostat that sent two thousand volts of electricity surging into Talap's body for seventeen seconds, followed quickly by a second jolt. At this point, Talap, who was knocked unconscious by the first blast, was examined by a team of doctors, who found that his pupils still reacted to light. After a brief third charge, Talap was pronounced dead.

E.A. Kell, a Pottstown doctor who attended both the execution and Talap's autopsy, reported that "every blood vessel in [Talap's] body burst with the entry of the charge" and that "his life ended instantaneously without suffering." Because there were no family or friends to claim his body, Talap was buried at the prison cemetery at Rockview, and an "unnamed Hungarian from Bridgeport" paid for the expenses.

Mary was buried next to her parents in the cemetery of St. John's Greek Catholic Church on North Hanover Street in Pottstown. Her stone is inscribed, "Mary, daughter of George and Mary Fesco." Her parents understandably eliminated the name of her murderer.

POTTSTOWN IN WORLD WAR I

At Home and Over There

On June 28, 1914, in the town of Sarajevo, Archduke Francis Ferdinand, heir to the throne of Austria-Hungary, and his wife, Princess Sophie, were shot to death by a Serbian nationalist. These assassinations were the catalyst that led to a world war that involved most of Europe and parts of the Near East as the Central Powers, consisting of Germany, Austria-Hungary, Bulgaria and Turkey, squared off against an Allied coalition that included Great Britain, France, Russia and Italy.

America avoided entering the war for four years, but on Good Friday, April 6, 1918, the United States of America officially declared war on the

German Empire. Pottstown's daily newspapers carried headlines such as "Wilson Declares War on Germany!" and "The United States Will Fight the Hun!"

Pottstonians were quick to show their support for their government. An organization called the Pottstown Protective League organized a mass meeting at the Grand Opera House that was held on April 23, during which "a grand outpouring of Pottstown citizens went on record in a pledge of lasting devotion." From start to finish, the people of Pottstown supported the war effort in every way possible, from buying war bonds to enduring the rationing of coal and a temporary ban on the selling of beer and liquor to donating peach pits to aid in manufacturing the carbon used in gas mask filters. (A note on the latter item: by early September, the "house wives of Pottstown" had donated 22,500 peach pits, from which enough carbon could be manufactured for 115 gas masks.)

The war put pressure on immigrants to show their loyalty to their new home, especially those who came from countries that were part of the Central Powers, such as Germany and Austria-Hungary. In Pottstown, they responded on July 8, 1918, with a parade, by which, according to the *Pottstown News*, "citizens of Foreign Birth Prove Loyalty." During this parade, "nearly 1,500 foreigners of Pottstown marched in a patriotic pageant on High Street." It must have been a stirring spectacle as these people marched down High Street accompanied by bands, carrying over one thousand American flags, as well as the flags of their native countries. The *News* especially mentioned the United Italians of Pottstown, who had 300 people in line led by Steve Fox, John Dore, James Bucholle and James Matto, and also the Greeks, led by William George and James George, who were 150 strong and had built a float that carried a model of a Liberty ship.

As spectacular as this parade was, it was upstaged by the Patriotic Loan Parade held on September 29, 1918, which had over five thousand participants and twenty bands and was so long that it took over an hour and a half to pass a given point. In this parade, the workers from each of the local industries marched as a unit. The McClintic-Marshall steel company contingent alone numbered twelve hundred, and included among it were "girls employed as crane operators and painters."

There is no official count of how many men from the Pottstown area fought against the Kaiser's army, but an examination of the Pottstown newspapers from that era makes an estimate of one thousand realistic.

Some Pottstown men didn't wait for the United States to declare war. In 1915, Richard Wilson, a forty-one-year-old plumber who lived at 647

Walnut Street, left his wife and children and went to Canada, where he joined the Forty-second Royal Highlanders, an infantry regiment known as the Black Watch. The plumber from Pottstown soon found himself fighting in the trenches in France, where he was wounded twice. Wilson, on temporary leave from the Canadian army, returned to Pottstown in May 1918. Not long after he returned to duty, he was discharged. The Canadians were finished with him, but Wilson wasn't ready to quit. On September 30, 1918, the *Ledger* reported that "Sergeant Richard H. Wilson…is now in the United States Army. He is 44 years of age and anxious for another scrap with the Hun."

Pottstown's National Guard unit became part of Company A of the 111th Infantry Regiment of the 28th Division, an outfit consisting entirely of Pennsylvania National Guard troops. The division was in almost continuous combat from July 1, 1918, until the Armistice on November 11, a little over four months later. On July 1, volunteers from Company A fought along with French infantry near Chateau Thierry. For their gallantry in this engagement, the French government awarded these men the Croix de Guerre with a palm.

It was here that Sergeant George "Red" Amole of 427 King Street became the first man from Pottstown to be killed in battle. Private Michael Vanish, son of Mr. and Mrs. Michael Vanish of 63 South Franklin Street, saw Amole go down and heard him say, "Boys, I got mine." Vanish also got his: a serious wound in his chest that left a hole "big enough to put your fist in," and another one in his left arm. While he lay helpless, he was hit by mustard gas, and a tree—hit by artillery—fell on his right leg. Mike Vanish survived and came back to Pottstown, where he spent the rest of his life.

On November 19, Sergeant James Gleason, another member of Company A, received the Distinguished Service Cross from General John Pershing for extraordinary heroism near Fishmette on August 9–12.

Pottstown native George Lehr was a guy who had everything going for him. Intelligent, handsome, good-natured and athletic, Lehr was the captain of the high school football team and senior class president. The son of German immigrants, he left his engineering studies at Penn State University to fight the Germans. A wound suffered in the Battle of Argonne cost him his left leg.

World War I saw the introduction of many "firsts," including the use of airplanes and poison gas. On July 11, 1918, Daniel Walter Brunish wrote to his mother, Mrs. Augusta Brunish of 608 Grant Street, "I wish you could see

George Amole, a sergeant in the Pottstown National Guard Company, was the first soldier from town killed in combat in World War I.

the aeroplanes do battle. They twist and squirm and dive and loop the loop, and keep banging away at each other. After a bit one will just flutter up there like a piece of paper and down he will come." Brunish was so enamored of these machines that he wished he "could go up in one of them. I'll bet it's thrilling. I think its got automobiling skinned to death."

Quite a few letters in the *News* mention poison gas. Pottstown resident David Keller of the Headquarters Company of the 111th Infantry wrote about two of his friends from town:

> *Bill Eckert and Cliff Wien were near me when a gas shell burst three feet away from us. Eckert was hit by some of the pieces. The three of us got the deadly effects of the gas. Eckert has since died. Wien and I were badly burnt by the gas which was mustard gas.*

Paul Binder, son of Mr. and Mrs. Mahlon Binder of 123 East Third Street, served in the French army as an ambulance driver and was at the front long before the Pottstown soldiers arrived. In a letter of August 12, Binder wrote to his mother about an attack with "machine guns pit-patting all around us and artillery swinging up the road at a gallop." According to Binder, "Our section [of ambulances] evacuated directly from the line for almost five days. We hauled 750 men the first day."

Binder described his new companion: "I am enclosing a picture of my pet monkey. His name is Ki-Ki. You can see him while I am driving, on the top

George Lehr (left) with two other wounded World War I soldiers at Camp Lee, New Jersey.

of the hood, fender or sitting on my shoulder. He likes it very much." The French government liked Paul Binder very much and thought so highly of his service that it awarded him the Croix de Guerre.

There were also many women who served as nurses in Europe during the war. Harriet L. Kulp, the twenty-one-year-old daughter of Mr. and Mrs. John

This float probably appeared in an Armistice Day Parade soon after 1918. *Courtesy of the Pottstown Historical Society.*

Kulp of 41 Hanover Street, was a 1917 graduate of the Pottstown Hospital Nursing School. Anxious to help, she volunteered for the Red Cross service and was sent to France. On October 18, 1918, she wrote to her parents, "I came over to help the boys and after being on duty just four days they put me to bed." Harriet had pneumonia, but she felt that she was getting better. She could sit up in bed and thought that she would soon be up and around. But that diagnosis was wishful thinking. On December 28, her parents received a telegram informing them of her death. Her desire to "help the boys" earned her a permanent resting place at the Shenkel United Church of Christ Cemetery across the Schuylkill from Pottstown in North Coventry Township.

George Kaas was Pottstown's "Last Man." On July 1, 1917, sixteen-year-old Kaas lied about his age so he could fight the Germans. During his stint, Kaas rescued his wounded lieutenant by crawling across one hundred yards of open ground under fire and carrying the man back to safety; a few weeks later, Kaas was seriously wounded. In 1938, Kaas and other local veterans formed a Last Man's Club and bought a bottle of cognac to be used by the last survivor to toast the memory of his comrades. Kaas won the cognac, but he refused to drink it and instructed his family to "give it to the boys at the Legion." He died on July 18, 1987.

On the west side of the Pottstown library is a monument whose inscription reads, "In Proud Remembrance of Pottstown Heroes Who Gave Their Lives in the Great World War for Freedom, Justice and Humanity." Above it are carved the names of the fifty-four men and women from Pottstown who died in World War I. They died in the war that was supposed to end all wars. Sadly, it didn't.

———•———

THE FLU EPIDEMIC OF 1918

The World's Deadliest Plague Visits Pottstown

For the citizens of Pottstown, in October 1918 it must have seemed that the world was coming to an end. Far away in France, the soldiers from town were involved in almost daily combat. Telegrams and letters were arriving bringing the news that someone was dead, wounded or sick.

At the same time, the town was in the grip of an influenza epidemic that was quickly killing scores of people. Those infected ran a high fever and usually developed pneumonia that could kill them within hours.

Known as the Spanish influenza, it is thought to have originated in Fort Riley, Kansas, where on March 11, 1918, just before breakfast, an army cook reported on sick call with a "bad cold." He was just the first raindrop at the beginning of the deluge. By noon, the camp surgeon had over one hundred sick men on his hands, all of them suffering with the same symptoms. After that, cases erupted everywhere.

At the end of August, the sickness popped up in the Boston area, where it quickly spread to nearby Camp Devens. Dr. Victor Vaughn, acting surgeon general of the army, went to Devens, where he saw "hundreds of young stalwart men in uniform coming into the wards of the hospital. Every bed was full, yet others crowded in." The symptoms that Dr. Vaughn observed were "faces [with] a bluish cast and a cough that brought up the blood-stained sputum." The next morning, the doctor noted, "Dead bodies are stacked about the morgue like cordwood."

On September 28, more than 200,000 people gathered in Philadelphia for a Liberty Loan Drive parade. Two days later, 635 new cases of influenza were reported there. The disease spread so rapidly throughout

Dr. Elmer Porter of Pottstown.
Courtesy of the Pottstown Historical Society.

the city that officials closed churches, schools, theatres and "all other public places of amusement."

At the same time the flu was ravishing Philadelphia, it was in Pottstown. On September 27, the family of George Shane was all but wiped out within one day as father, mother and one son died within twenty-four hours of one another. The only survivor was twelve-year-old Charles Shane, who was sent to live with his grandmother in Berwick, Pennsylvania.

On October 4, Dr. Elmer J. Porter, president of Pottstown's Board of Health, reported that the "epidemic has reached alarming proportions in the borough within the last few days." Of course, the medical profession had no weapons in its arsenal that could combat the disease once a person was infected, but doctors and public health officials were positive that the flu was spread from person to person, so they published in the Pottstown newspapers a list of steps to follow to avoid being infected. Some of them made sense: avoid crowds, wash your hands frequently and keep your home clean and well ventilated. However, some of their nostrums were

The Pottstown Hospital during the 1918 flu epidemic. *Courtesy of the Pottstown Historical Society.*

a little strange, such as "take a handful of lukewarm milk and snuffle up your nose and retain it awhile until the milk works into the tissues." In addition to that, people were advised to "chew juniper berries that are in good condition." Meanwhile, a lady from Portland, Oregon, reported that she cured her four-year-old daughter from the flu by dosing her with onion syrup and burying her from head to toe for three days in glistening raw onions.

Pottstown officials, like those in Philadelphia, gradually closed down many public gathering places. The schools were closed on October 4, and then churches stopped holding services; finally, the Commonwealth of Pennsylvania ordered all public places closed, including theatres, bars and soda fountains. These actions probably saved many lives, but the disease was still holding high carnival in Pottstown.

The paper reported on October 4 that fifteen to eighteen hundred people were already infected. From that point on, every day's edition had mortality reports on the front page. On October 7 it was reported that four people had died during the last forty-eight hours. On Monday, October 18, as the disease swung into high gear, it was reported that there had been seventeen deaths in the community over the weekend.

Near the end of the month, the infection was so extensive that many of the town's services were affected. The trolley service was "severely crippled," the staff at the post office suffered six deaths in twenty-four hours, the telephone company requested that because of an "increasing shortage of operators, all subscribers" refrain from making calls not required by "sickness, war work, or absolute necessity."

Even the staff at Pottstown Hospital was so hard hit that it was requesting volunteers to work both the day and night shifts. Also hard hit were the town's industries, with so many of the workers ill that most of the plants were shut down. Under normal conditions, Pottstown was a busy community, but during those few weeks in October the streets were probably relatively empty.

The newspaper headlines were sometimes a trifle lurid. "Grim Reaper Continues to Take Toll While Epidemic Rages Here" was plastered across the front page of the October 11 edition of the *Pottstown News*, and the paper also noted that "there was little rest these days for the local undertaker."

Fortunately, the flu's visit was short. By the beginning of November, the disease was on the wane, fewer new cases were being reported and the churches were allowed to reopen. By November 7, the *News* reported, "Business is normal as the flu ban is lifted," and "there was no rush at the bars after being closed for 4 weeks."

There is no exact count of the number of fatalities in Pottstown during the epidemic. On October 23, it was reported that the flu had claimed 124 victims dating back to September 26, but there was never a final number published in any of Pottstown's three newspapers. Perhaps the best information can be gleaned from the *Pottstown Daily Ledger*'s necrology that was published in early January 1919. According to those figures, 299 adults and 73 children died in Pottstown from September to the end of November, totaling 372 deaths.

Given the virulence of the disease, it is probably safe to assume that it was the cause of almost all of these deaths, which means that almost 3 percent of the town's population died in the outbreak. But these figures do not include the men and women from Pottstown who died of the flu while in federal service, and given the contagious nature of the disease, there were certainly at least a few.

Recent research shows that the flu virus was probably passed from birds to pigs and then to humans, like the Asian flu of 1957 and the Hong Kong flu of 1968. It started in the United States and quickly became a pandemic that decimated populations throughout the world. Within eighteen months, it disappeared as quickly as it had come. It was so malignant that during its short reign it is estimated that it caused anywhere from twenty-five to thirty-seven million deaths, which makes it the most deadly disease in the history of mankind.

Part IV

POTTSTOWN AT MID-CENTURY

WORLD WAR II MAKES ITS MARK

December 7, 1941, was a typical Sunday afternoon for nineteen-year-old Gabe Fieni and his buddies as they lounged in front of his parents' neighborhood grocery store and restaurant at No. 1 West Fourth Street. But the idyllic scene changed abruptly when Ed Pyote came running down the middle of the street shouting, "Pearl Harbor was bombed by the Japs!" At first, the guys were nonplussed by the news. "Where in the hell is Pearl Harbor?" someone asked. "When we found out," Fieni said, "we went from happy-go-lucky to real angry almost instantly."

The Japanese surprise air attack that Sunday on the U.S. Navy's Pacific Fleet docked at Pearl Harbor was the catalyst that sent America into World War II and would scatter over four thousand men and women from the Pottstown area to all parts of the world.

The attack on Pearl Harbor was the end of the war for Lieutenant Commander Daniel R. Fox of the United States Marine Corps, who was one of the 1,177 killed aboard the USS *Arizona* that morning. Fox, who grew up in Pottstown, joined the U.S. Marines as a private in 1916. During his career, he received eleven medals and decorations, including the Distinguished Service Cross for gallantry in World War I. Fox was the first person from Pottstown to die in World War II, and somebody had to be the last. That sad distinction goes to Anthony Marchione, who was not only the last man from the borough to be killed but also the last man to be killed in air combat in the entire war. Born in Pottstown in 1925, Marchione joined the U.S. Army Air Corps in 1943 and eventually became an assistant photographer who took part in aerial reconnaissance. On July 18, 1945, five days after Japan surrendered, the young airman was the member of a crew that flew over Tokyo to test Japan's compliance with the surrender agreement. During that mission, Japanese Zeros attacked Marchione's airplane, and one of their rounds punched into the plane and hit him in the chest. He died a few minutes later. Buried in Okinawa, his body was brought home in 1949 and reinterred at the old St. Aloysius Cemetery on High Street.

There were so many from the area who served during World War II that it is impossible to tell all of their stories. However, in February 1943, 163 men from the Pottstown area were invited by Uncle Sam to join the United States Army. A number of them wound up in the 104th Infantry Regiment, which was part of the 26th Division, well known as the Yankee Division in General George S. Patton's 3rd Army.

Five of these men—Ed Dobry, Morris "Spike" Gauger, Tom Bondola, Paul Reigner and Stanley Davidheiser—were captured by the Germans in October 1944 and shipped to Germany, where they were put to work at an air base repairing damage caused by Allied bombing raids. The men had to subsist on a diet that consisted mostly of stale black bread and watery soup—starvation rations that eventually killed some of them. Ed Dobry lost about 60 pounds. "I was lucky," he recalled. "I weighed about 170 when I was captured, but some of the smaller fellows didn't have much weight to give away." On May 3, 1945, Dobry, Davidheiser and Gauger were liberated by the Russians and eventually shipped back to the United States. After the war, all of them returned to Pottstown, where they prospered, and at the time of this writing three are still alive.

Pottstown native Willard Bickel, also a member of this group, became the sergeant major of the 3rd Battalion of the 104th. Bickel married Margaret Robenolt of Pottstown just before he was drafted. "I said 'I do' to Margaret on February 13 and 'I do' to Uncle Sam on the fifteenth, and on February 22 I was on my way."

Pottstown soldier Edward Dobry with his mother, Anna, at the family home, 425 South Street. *Courtesy of Edward Dobry.*

He was on his way, but not without Margaret, who accompanied him to all of his basic training camps. "There were nine of us girls that went," she recalled, and "when they moved, we moved." Typically, the wives would get to an area before their husbands to locate housing, which was very difficult to find. Because Margaret was a skilled bookkeeper, she could always find work, including a job with a candy company in Augusta, Georgia.

With thousands of the town's young men away in the service, Pottstown seemed deserted. At least, it did in the south end of town, where William "Pappy" Spang had a little grocery store at the corner of Cherry and Franklin Streets. Spang's, the neighborhood hangout, was always a lively place, but during the war, one south ender remembers it as a "pathetic site," as "all the guys were gone."

When World War II began, Congress and the military were very reluctant to allow women in the service—the exception being the Army and Navy Nurses Corps, organized in 1901 and 1908, respectively. However, by early 1942, the mounting manpower crisis made it necessary to bring women into the military. On March 15, Congress created the Women's Auxiliary Army Corps (WAAC), and on July 30, the navy's Women Accepted for Volunteer Emergency Service (WAVES) came into being. In these organizations and several others, more than 400,000 women served in the armed forces during World War II. Scanning the *Pottstown Mercury* for the years 1942 and 1945 revealed the names of 18 women from the Pottstown area who served in one these organizations, but no doubt there were more.

One such woman, Geraldine Leblang, a daughter of Mrs. Sarah Leblang of 429 High Street, served in the WAAC and after the war became the secretary to the state adjutant of Disabled American Veterans of California. (Her brother, Raymond, who joined the U.S. Navy in 1940, was killed in action in November 1942.) Army nurse Lieutenant Elisabeth Galloway was the first woman from Pottstown to be sent on overseas duty. She wired her dad on Fathers Day 1942 to say that she had arrived safely in Australia.

Ironically, World War II caused the American economy to boom as the country's industry had to meet the demands of the Allied military forces. This was certainly the case in Pottstown, where scores of plants operated around the clock. The need for workers attracted people from as far away as Lancaster, Bethlehem and the coal regions, so by 1943 the borough's population had jumped to 20,194. The upsurge triggered a spike in home construction so that, despite the shortage of raw materials, houses were built in the east and north ends of town. One of these projects was

Geraldine Leblang served in the WAAC during World War II. *Courtesy of the Pottstown Historical Society.*

Hilldale—210 apartments built with federal money in 1943 to house all of the temporary workers pouring into town. Built just east of the borough line in Lower Pottsgrove Township, Hilldale was located around the area that now encompasses the Armand Hammer Boulevard entrance ramp to U.S. 422. Hilldale was scheduled to be torn down as soon as the war ended, but a severe postwar housing shortage prolonged its life until 1953. No trace of it remains today.

The war removed economic anxiety in Pottstown but replaced it with a new kind: anxiety for the thousands of family and friends fighting overseas. Would they return safely home? On December 23, the editor of the *Mercury* asked the question foremost in everyone's minds: "I wonder how many of us will be together next Christmas Eve."

Twenty months later, on the night of August 13–14, 1945, NBC Radio broadcast a performance by Cab Callaway and his band from Zanzibar in Manhattan. Almost every home in Pottstown had a radio set, so it is quite possible that some area night owls were listening to the music when, at 1:15 a.m. on the fourteenth, an announcer cut into the program with the news that the Japanese government had officially agreed to surrender. World War II was over. The news of the war's end reached most of Pottstown's citizens at 7:00 p.m. that day, when air raid sirens and church bells cut loose; the cacophony was a catharsis that released the years of worry, tension and grief. One York Street resident recalled the din. "I didn't know what it meant," she said, but it "brought everybody out into the street." At first, no one knew what it signified, but then word spread, and soon people were cheering and singing. "I cried for happiness. They were tears of joy."

The *Mercury* reported that on High Street "Pottstonians [went] Wild... Torn paper poured over High Street from the upper stories of buildings and passing cars." The crowd rapidly swelled into the thousands as "persons rushed in all directions towards the center of activities." The din made normal conversation impossible as cars, bicycles, motorcycles and trucks loaded with cheering people cruised down the main drag, along with fire engines and ambulances with blaring sirens. "Cow bells clanged, tin cans rattled, cap pistols went off, bugles sounded, and four airplanes roared overhead." One man stood at the corner of High and Hanover Streets waving the same American flag that he had displayed twenty-seven years before at the close of World War I, while at the same corner another man was "dressed as a woman with a white bow attached to a comb in his hair, pink undergarments and high heeled shoes."

During World War II, at least 4,023 area men and women served in the armed forces; 72 of them died, and many more were wounded.

DR. ALICE E. SHEPPARD

"The Most Useful Woman in Town"

People born before 1950 remember when their family doctor made house calls. The following is a story about one of these visits that ended with a flourish that makes even the mostly kindly general practitioner look like a misanthrope. One day, a Pottstown housewife with three young children suddenly became very ill. It was nothing serious—probably the flu—but it hit her hard enough that she was temporarily out of commission. She called the family doctor, who came to her house, examined her and gave her some medicine. Then, looking around, the doctor noticed some dishes in the sink. "You lay back and rest. I'll take care of these for you." Fifteen or twenty minutes later, the dishes were washed and dried, and the doctor was on her way to her next patient. That doctor was Alice E. Sheppard, and that act of kindness—"TLC," she liked to call it—was an integral part of her way of practicing family medicine.

Dr. Sheppard, the fourth and youngest child of George Q. and Mary (Keim) Sheppard, was born on March 9, 1898, in the Sheppards' home at 722 King Street. Her father taught mathematics at the Hill School for forty-five years and was active in Pottstown civic affairs, serving several terms on the school board and for many years as deacon of the First Presbyterian Church. Her mother was also very active in community affairs, with many years of service on the board of directors of the Pottstown Hospital and the Century Club, as well as teaching Sunday school at the First Presbyterian Church.

The Sheppards placed a high premium on education, so at fourteen, Alice began a three-year stint in boarding schools. In 1915, she enrolled in Mount Holyoke College, where it appears she was successful both academically and socially, as she announced to her mother in a letter of May 19, 1916: "We had a class meeting Thursday afternoon to elect next year's officers and I was elected president. Imagine!"

After receiving her BA from Mount Holyoke in 1919, Sheppard returned to Pottstown and took a teaching position at the Wyndcroft School. As she later recalled, "I taught arithmetic and geography. Didn't know a thing about them."

What Alice knew was that she wanted to be a medical doctor. She went into the study of medicine well aware that the attendant difficulties involved in becoming a licensed doctor would be much harder for her because she was a woman in an era when there was still a very strong prejudice against women even aspiring to enter the profession. Undaunted, she accepted the challenge, merely saying almost thirty years later, "I wanted to do it, so I did."

In 1920, Sheppard moved to New York City, where she spent two years working by day at Columbia University in the laboratory of the noted zoologist Dr. Edmund Beecher Wilson while she took the math and science courses required for admission to medical school at Columbia's night school. With her math and science prerequisites satisfied, in 1922 Sheppard began her pursuit of the doctorate of medicine at the Women's Medical College of Pennsylvania (now Drexel University's College of Medicine) in Philadelphia.

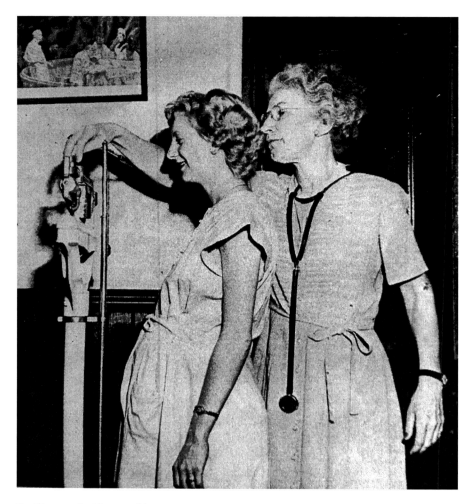

Dr. Sheppard with one of her many maternity patients. *Courtesy of the Library of Congress.*

Upon her graduation from Women's Medical, in 1926 the newly minted doctor served a year's internship at Lancaster General Hospital in Lancaster, Pennsylvania, and followed that with a term as medical director of the Women's Hospital in Philadelphia.

In 1928, Sheppard returned to Pottstown to practice medicine. The prospect of being the only female doctor in town caused the normally intrepid Sheppard to be "fearful that some of the men physicians might be hostile."

On October 15, Dr. Sheppard opened her first office at 14 North Franklin Street and waited. More than twenty years later, she still vividly remembered the first patient's arrival—a lady who was an old friend of her family. "When I looked out of my office into the waiting room and saw her, I was so rattled that I called out 'Are you a patient?' I couldn't believe I had one."

For the next forty years, Dr. Sheppard practiced family medicine and obstetrics in Pottstown, saw patients in her office, in their homes and at the Pottstown Hospital and, during that time, delivered 2,010 babies. She seemed to have set no limits on the amount of time she devoted to her patients. "Of course you can call me on Sundays," she was often heard to tell a patient. Her home telephone number was listed, and so people called. At any hour of the day or night, no matter how harsh the weather, she could be seen walking to her car parked at the rear of the family home.

In addition to her practice, she taught at the Pottstown Hospital's School of Nursing, was chief of obstetrics and served a term as the medical staff president. She was active in her professional association, serving terms as president and secretary of the Montgomery County Medical Association, and also held office in the Pennsylvania State Medical Association. In town, Dr. Sheppard was active in many civic and charitable groups, including the Salvation Army, the Red Cross, the American Cancer Society, the Business and Professional Women's Club, the Visiting Nurses Association and the United Way.

In 1949, the hardworking doctor had a moment in the national spotlight when *Look*, a well-known biweekly magazine with a circulation of three million, did a three-page photographic article on her in its December 20 edition. Chosen because the editors thought she was "representative of the nation's 10,000 women physicians," the article began, "In Pottstown, Pennsylvania, they call Alice Sheppard, M.D. 'the most useful woman in town.'"

Of course, everyone was impressed; that is, except for Dr. Sheppard, who modestly told a *Mercury* reporter that she "didn't know what all the fuss was about. There are dozens of women in town doing as much or more than I do and we have three other good women physicians." Privately, her response to the article was less diplomatic. She confided to her nephew in a letter of November 29:

The Look *business is driving me slowly mad. Now I understand they are circularizing all Pottstown and enclosing a note that the article about me will appear in the December 20th issue which hits the newsstands on December 6th and what is the worst part is that they say I am the only woman doctor in Pottstown. Do my colleagues love that! I will probably have to appear on the Broadcast from Norristown that day which features Pottstown news. I certainly didn't realize what I was letting myself in for. AND I FEEL LIKE A NUT! Fortunately the public's memory is very short-lived and I will sink back into my usual rut very quickly.*

Following the *Look* feature, more awards came her way. On October 4, 1952, her alma mater, Mount Holyoke College, presented her with a citation for "her service to society" during its two-day convocation on science and human values. On October 14, 1958, the Pennsylvania State Medical Society, at its annual meeting in Philadelphia, named Sheppard the society's "general practitioner of 1958 for her outstanding and devoted service to medicine and to her community, county and state." The first woman to receive the award, the doctor modestly tried to deflect the attention from herself, stating that "most of the credit must go to her associates in the Montgomery County Medical Society and the people of Pottstown."

The attention didn't disturb Dr. Sheppard's focus on her practice; she continued to work at her usual frenetic pace. Eventually, her body gave way under the strain of her schedule. On August 16, one month after delivering her 2,000th baby, she suffered a massive heart attack. The blow was severe enough that she could not resume her former schedule. From that point on, there would be no more house calls, no more setting out at 3:00 a.m. to deliver a baby. She could see patients in her office or at the hospital.

Dr. Sheppard retired a few years later, on July 1, 1968. She said "she would miss the activity of the profession and the feeling of well-being derived from helping others." But she admitted that "time had caught up with her." For the next few years, she was still very active. She informed friends from her Mount Holyoke days, "With numerable meetings of Church, United Fund, Salvation Army, etc., I have little time to wonder how to keep busy."

Dr. Alice Sheppard died of heart failure on July 3, 1972. Three days later, "A Gracious Lady" appeared on the editorial page of the *Mercury*. It was a eulogy to Dr. Sheppard, pointing out that her dedication, knowledge and understanding made her a great doctor; it also stated that she was "more interested in her patients' well being than in her own" and for that "they loved her." In conclusion, the editor wrote that "Pottstown was a better place" because of her.

AL GREY, WORLD-CLASS JAZZ TROMBONIST

"I'm Going Out There and I'm Gonna Make It"

Albert Thornton Grey was the third child of Richard Grey and his wife, Lucy Ann Green. Al was born in Aldie, Virginia, on June 6, 1925, and became a citizen of Pottstown four months later when the family moved to the borough. Al's love for music came from his father, who was a bugler in the army during World War I and played the trumpet. Al told his friend Bob Bernotas, a freelance jazz writer from Manhattan, "I started playing at

Al Grey with a few of his many trombones. *Courtesy of the* Pottstown Mercury.

the age of four, cause I was messin' with my father's trumpet." Then with a chuckle, he said, "I used to get spankings for messin' with it." Even though his father didn't want Al "messin'" with his trumpet, he gave Al his first music lessons and his first experience at playing in a band.

Al played baritone horn and the sousaphone, but his love for the trombone came from listening to his band director, Pottstown native Harvey Leroy Wilson, play that instrument. Later, Al told a *Mercury* reporter:

> *I learned to play all kinds music around here. In Pottstown, when I was in junior high school, we used to play polkas in the fire house down on Franklin Street (the Empire Hook and Ladder Company). We also used to go to the homes of different kids we knew, and the parents would fix cookies for us if we would play something for them. I knew right then I wanted to be a musician.*

A child of the 1930s, Al loved jazz, but in his words, "We were a religious family and I couldn't play jazz at the house." However, he did play it away from home. Arlen Saylor, who later played cornet with the United States Army Band, remembers that he and Al and a few other student musicians started a jazz band and rehearsed at St. John's Byzantine Catholic Church. Saylor recalled that "even then Al had a good feeling for jazz, and he was our jazz player."

Al left high school in 1944 and joined the navy. He was sent to the Great Lakes Naval Training Center, where he devoted his time to mastering the trombone, practicing in "the head" until he was good enough to join band. The navy eventually sent Al to Grosse Isle Naval Station near Detroit. He recalled, "I used to come into Detroit and go jammin' at the nightclubs. They used to call me 'the Sailor Boy.' They didn't know my name but they said, 'The Sailor Boy comes around and he plays pretty good.'"

His playing in Detroit was so impressive that three days after his discharge from the navy, he was hired to play in Benny Carter's band. For the rest of his life, Al Grey was a jazz trombonist. In addition to Benny Carter, he played with Lucky Milander, Lionel Hampton, Dizzy Gillespie and, between 1957 and 1977, three stints with Count Basie. In between his band work were sandwiched other things: for a while in the late 1940s he had his own band in Texas; in the early '50s he played studio work in New York City.

Through his recordings with Count Basie, he developed, as Bob Bernotas wrote, "a reputation as a unique solo voice and a sensitive accompanist," which led to recording dates with top singers such as Ella Fitzgerald, Sarah Vaughn, Frank Sinatra, Bing Crosby, Tony Bennett and Ray Charles. From 1961, except for episodes with Basie, Al was a freelance artist, "heading up a string of swinging combos" that, since 1988, included his son, Michael Grey, on trombone.

Despite his nomadic lifestyle, Grey maintained a connection with his family and Pottstown. When he was with Basie, Al would invite the entire band to his parents' house for some home cooking when they came to town to play at Sunnybrook. "Al was very proud of my mom," his brother said, "so he would bring 'em home." Lucy Grey, always equal to the challenge, made them dinner while Count Basie sat in the kitchen and watched her cook.

After his parents were gone, Al bought their house in Stowe to use as a retreat where he could recharge his batteries and sometimes go to Sunnybrook Ballroom to sit in with his old friend Arlen Saylor's band. As he told a *Mercury* reporter in 1985, "Traveling as much as I do, I haven't found any other place that makes me feel comfortable living for a while."

In 1944, when Al was getting ready to leave Pottstown for the navy, he told his sister, "Jen, you can stay here and play your hymns and anthems and classicals and all, but I'm going out there and I'm gonna make it!" Al Grey made it bigger than even he could have dreamt at the time. His musicianship and ebullient personality won the hearts and respect of everyone, from greats like Frank Sinatra to jazz audiences all over the world. After he died on March 24, 2000, Bob Bernotas wrote, "The entire music world lost one of its all-time greats."

The Good Will Boys Band of Pottstown

Richard Grey Sr., Al's father, was born on March 17, 1892, in Aldie, Virginia. He loved music, played the trumpet and was a bugler in the U.S. Army during World War I. After the war, he married Miss Lucy Ann Green, a schoolteacher with a warm personality and a smile that could light up an entire room.

Lucy, although raised by her grandmother in the Aldie area, was born in Pottstown and had family there. After the war, good jobs were scarce in Aldie, so in 1925, the Greys moved to Pottstown, where they felt they could make a better home for their children.

The Good Will Boys Band of Pottstown in the 1930s. Al Grey is holding the tuba. *Courtesy of the Pottstown Historical Society.*

Richard Grey began teaching his children to play as soon as they were big enough to hold an instrument. Richard Jr. played clarinet, Al was on baritone and Jenny started on clarinet but was switched to cornet. Richard, who now lives in Reading, no longer plays, Al's musical feats are well known and Jenny, now Mrs. Jenny Beck of Mount Airy, plays the trumpet, piano and organ and is the assistant minister of music at the Enon Tabernacle Baptist Church in Philadelphia. Richard and Lucy Grey's eldest child, Naomi, died in Pottstown in the 1920s, and her parents raised her daughter, Ella, who is now the wife of Joseph Miller of Pottstown.

In 1930, Grey organized the Good Will Band. "Good Will meant good will for everybody," Richard Grey Jr. proclaimed. "Even Gibble [a local sign painter] painted the drum head for very little. It was part of the good will." He began teaching the children who wanted to join. Richard and Lucy Grey built that band from nothing. By working extra hours at Lamb's Music Store, they earned money to buy music, music stands and many of the instruments that the boys played. Frank Schatz, who owned a small cigar factory on North Charlotte Street and had been the director of the Boyertown Keystone Band, supplied the group with uniforms and helped the elder Grey to improve his knowledge of music. He also gave Richard Jr. clarinet lessons.

One of the band's first jobs was playing in the victory parade that Pottstown's Democrats held after Franklin Roosevelt won his first presidential election in 1932. Richard Grey still remembers it:

> *We drove on High Street, it was cold, and we were sitting on benches in the back of Mr. Yost's* [James Yost of 728 Lincoln Avenue] *truck playing "Happy Days Are Here Again." We went as far as Gilbertsville and Boyertown. That was big times!*

The intrepid Grey was willing to take the band anywhere. In Yost's truck, they made forays into the coal regions and as far as "back home in Virginia." Most of their playing, however, was at church festivals and block parties along Beech and Walnut Streets. Half of the money earned was divided among the boys and the other half invested in the band.

The advent of the Civilian Conservation Camps in the late '30s and World War II siphoned off the players and brought about the band's demise. For a decade, the Good Will Boys Band was a fixture in Pottstown. Older residents still remember its performances. One recalled, "It was amazing the sound he got from those boys." According to Mrs. Margaret Ricketts, who has been observing life in Pottstown for the past ninety years, "Mr. Grey loved and spent a lot of time with kids…He deserves great credit."

The end of the band was not the end of Richard Grey's efforts. He maintained a small studio at his home in Stowe, where he continued to teach children into the last years of his life. Richard Grey died in Pottstown Hospital on December 19, 1978. His wife, Lucy Ann, died at their home in Stowe on October 19, 1962. They are buried at Oak Grove Cemetery in Parkerford.

HOMETOWN PEOPLE WHO MADE GOOD

Residents of a small community like Pottstown always take pride in hearing about one of their own going out into the world and being successful. On that note, the following vignettes are about four of the many noteworthy people who called Pottstown home.

JOHN EAGLE, a son of Conrad and Mary (Kane Eagle), was born on July 23, 1868, near Pine Forge in Berks County. Two years later, the Eagles moved to Pottstown, where they lived at 359 Chestnut Street. In 1912, a Pottstown newspaper wrote that Eagle left Pottstown "while still a high school boy then went to Paterson, New Jersey where he studied law and then went into silk manufacturing." Eagle got his start in the early 1890s by investing in a silk mill in Shamokin, Pennsylvania. His younger brother Charles joined him in the business, and the two turned the Shamokin mill into a wonderfully successful operation that, just after the turn of the century, was capitalized at $20 million.

The Eagle brothers expanded their business, eventually acquiring five mills in Pennsylvania, including one in Phoenixville and another in New Jersey. Their company's headquarters was at a modest location in Manhattan until 1912, when it was transferred to a "million-dollar skyscraper" that the brothers had built on Fourth Avenue.

The Eagle Company was international in scope, buying raw silk in China and Japan and then bringing it to its factories in America, where it was made into finished fabric and then sold to buyers worldwide. At the height of its success in the early 1920s, it employed twelve thousand workers and had an annual payroll of $6 million.

In 1922, John Eagle sold his share to his brother Charles, retired and moved to Pasadena, California. He spent the rest of his life traveling the world and hunting big game in Africa. He enjoyed another twenty-one years of living *la dolce vita* and died on July 23, 1943, his seventy-fifth birthday. In his will, he left $7 million to his wife and siblings, $5,000 to the Pottstown YMCA and $2,500 to the Pottstown Salvation Army. Today, his estate in Pasadena is the home of the Mayfield Independent School, a college preparatory school for young women founded by the Society of the Holy Child Jesus.

Pottstown native WILLIAM F. LAMB JR. was well known around town as a professional-caliber musician, businessman and music educator. The son of William F. Lamb Sr. and his wife, Viola Missimer, he was born at his parents' home, 269 Chestnut Street, on October 31, 1915. William Lamb Sr., the owner of a very successful music store in town, was also a church organist and director of the Pottstown Band, and it was through his influence that Bill began playing the cornet when he was six years old.

William F. Lamb Jr. as the conductor of the Pottstown Band, circa 1960.

Lamb rapidly developed into an outstanding player and by the mid-1920s had become a seasoned performer, appearing on live radio broadcasts from Philadelphia and New York and before large audiences. When he was twelve, he made a solo appearance with the then famous Giuseppe Creatore and his band at the Steel Pier in Atlantic City. A year later, Lamb performed for six thousand people in Philadelphia. In the first half of the concert, he played cornet solos backed up by a sixty-five-piece band, and in the second half he played marimba solos accompanied on the piano by his father.

During World War II, Lamb was the solo cornetist with the United States Army Band for four years. Following that, he returned to Pottstown to work in the music store that he later owned.

After the war, Bill concentrated on conducting. He took over the Pottstown Band and, together with his wife, Margaret Reid Lamb, transformed it into a stylish, upbeat outfit complemented by a chorus and vocal soloists that played custom arrangements of modern songs, as well as the traditional band repertoire. In 1950, the *Mercury* noted that "the Pottstown Band with young Billy Lamb measuring the downbeats, still is thrilling the music lovers in the groves these summer days."

In 1963, Lamb began organizing the Pottstown Symphony and stepped down as the conductor of the Pottstown Band, turning the reins over to Arlen Saylor. In May 1964, a little over a year later, the Pottstown Symphony, thanks to the energy of William Lamb, made its debut. Lamb remained its principal conductor until illness forced him to step down in 1982.

In 1968, Bill left the store and became the supervisor of the Pottstown School District's music department and conductor of the high school band.

Lamb died at his home in Gilbertsville, Pennsylvania, on June 6, 1982. During his life, he gave Pottstown pride with his playing and the transformation of the Pottstown Band, and he left the community the marvelous legacies of the Pottstown Symphony and a strong public school music program.

HARVEY LEE WILSON is another home-grown musician who accomplished much. The son of Harvey and Lettie Wilson, he was born in Pottstown on June 3, 1913, at his parents' home at 172 North Charlotte Street. Wilson grew up studying the trombone, and by the time he graduated from Pottstown High School in 1931, he played so well that he won admission to the Curtis Institute of Music in Philadelphia, one of the most prestigious and selective music conservatories in the world.

For a few years in the early 1930s, Wilson had his own band—the house band at Sunny Brook—and then later taught instrumental music for the Pottstown School District. After serving in World War II, he earned a doctorate in music education at the University of Pennsylvania and then set out on a distinguished career as a teacher, composer and conductor.

After he retired in 1983, Harvey returned to Pottstown, where he died in 1994. In his will, Wilson left two large legacies to the Pottstown School District: the Harvey Lee Wilson Scholarship Fund, which pays tuition for Pottstown High School graduates who are going on to college to study music, and the Phoebe Sime Trust Fund, named in honor of his sister, which annually allocates money to promote music at Pottstown High School.

ANNE ESTELLE RICE, the fourth child of James Kennedy and Emmeline (Fegley) Rice, was born on June 11, 1877, in Ringtown, a tiny village a few miles northwest of Shenandoah in Schuylkill County, Pennsylvania. In 1884, James Rice brought his family to Pottstown, where Anne grew up and went to school.

Anne Estelle Rice, photo taken about 1898. *From* The Expressive Fauvism of Anne Estelle Rice, *by Dr. Carol Nathanson.*

Rice left Pottstown in 1894 to study illustration and art at the School of Industrial Art of the Pennsylvania Museum in Philadelphia and remained in the city to pursue her career. During the next few years, her work appeared in well-known magazines of the time such as *Collier's, Harper's Bazaar,* the *Ladies Home Journal* and the *Saturday Evening Post.* Her work drew the attention of Thomas Wanamaker, owner of the Philadelphia newspaper *North American,* and in 1905 he sent her to Paris to illustrate the latest in women's fashions for the Wannamaker Department Stores.

After two years in Paris, Rice shifted her focus from illustration to painting. Her talent was quickly recognized by critics, who described her canvases as "expansive" and "strikingly bold in color" and praised her style as "vigorous and personal, her methods definite and unhesitating."

In 1909, Anne Rice's success in Europe earned her a commission in America. John Wanamaker, who was in the process of razing his old store in Philadelphia and building a new one, hired Rice to do a series of murals. The artist worked on the project for four years, creating seven large canvases that, when hung, spanned almost the entire width of the Market Street side of the store.

In 1913, the young artist married Raymond Drey, an English art critic whom she met in Paris. She and Drey settled in London, and in 1919 they had a son, David. Although she remained devoted to painting and produced many excellent works, her career, when compared to its rocketing trajectory during her Paris years, went into decline. She died in her sleep in a London hospital on September 20, 1959.

Over the last ten years, there has been a marked revival of interest in Anne Rice's work. In 1997, the Hollis Taggart Art Galleries in New York City mounted a large exhibit of her paintings titled The Expressive Fauvism of Anne Estelle Rice. An Internet survey of art auctions also shows a rising demand for Rice's paintings; for example, a sale held by Sotheby's Art Auction House in August 2008 featured five of them, with several expected to go under the hammer for as high as £60,000 (at that time, the equivalent of over $100,000).

In 2007, the Brooklyn Museum acquired one of Rice's most highly acclaimed pieces, *The Egyptian Dancers*, which had been missing for more than sixty years. The painting is considered to be "among the most significant achievements by an American modernist, or by an American woman at work among the turn-of-the-century Parisian avant-garde."

HURRICANE AGNES PUMMELS POTTSTOWN

"You're Never Too Old to Begin Again"

National disasters are events that are supposed to take place somewhere else. The network news shows you snippets of a small midwestern town being washed away by the flooding of the Mississippi River, or you watch a National Geographic special on the eruption of Mount St. Helens and shudder as survivors tell stories of how they escaped death. So when Mother Nature spins her wheel and your number comes up, at first it is as if you are watching it happen to someone else.

That is probably the way some people in Pottstown felt when the flood of the century came to their town on Friday, June 23, 1972. The trouble was brought by Hurricane Agnes, a storm that, from June 19 to 24, dropped as much as nineteen inches of rain as it roared out of the Gulf of Mexico and hit every state from Florida to New York, forcing 210,000 people to flee their homes, killing 117 and causing $32 billion in damage. The National

Two men rescue a resident of the south end of Pottstown during Hurricane Agnes. *Courtesy of the* Pottstown Mercury.

Weather Service ranks Agnes as "the nation's 2nd most destructive national disaster," but in Pennsylvania, where it killed 50 people and caused $2.3 billion in damages, it is still number one.

Conditions were ripe for this event. A cold spring and a cool, wet June kept runoff conditions high. But when the rain began on Thursday the twenty-second, few people in Pottstown were worried, and they went about their normal daily routines. However, by noon the waters of the Schuylkill River and the Manatawny Creek were creeping over their banks, and it was obvious that there would be flooding.

The town began to mobilize as businesses and factories began closing, and policemen, firemen and rescue workers were put on alert. Still, the flood became critical much faster than anybody anticipated. Anthony Mosera, owner of the Down Town Motor Inn at High and Manatawny Streets, was incredulous at how quickly the waters rose, recalling that "at 11:00 a.m. there was just a few inches of water at the curb; by 3:00 p.m. the Inn was flooded."

The rapidly rising water trapped many people. Two Philadelphia Electric workers were marooned in the company's substation just upstream from

A helicopter rescue of Pottstown residents during Hurricane Agnes. *Courtesy of the* Pottstown Mercury.

the Hanover Street Bridge. Initial efforts to rescue them only succeeded in creating more "rescuees" when a motorboat carrying four people and a canoe with two both capsized while trying to reach the stranded workers. Now there were eight people in the water holding on for dear life to trees and utility poles. It took an hour until they were all brought to safety. One of the workers gasped with relief, "It felt like four hours. When we found out we couldn't swim in the water we just grabbed hold. I grabbed a telegraph pole. Most of the others grabbed trees."

Some people in South Pottstown were in grave danger. A short distance south of the river the land rises very steeply, and this forced the floodwaters into a small channel where their depth and power were magnified. Many of the people whose homes were in that narrow strip of lowland were trapped with night coming on, the rain still driving and the river rising fast. Some managed to get out by boat, but the current was now moving so fast that "even fifty-horsepower motors couldn't make headway."

Locally, there were no resources that were capable of rescuing the stranded, but fortunately help was on its way.

The heroes in this situation were the men of the Helicopter Combat Support Squadron No. 21948 from the Willow Grove Naval Air Station. That afternoon, these teams began arriving at Pottstown Municipal Airport and, after being briefed, took off for South Pottstown to begin their mission. Frank E. Sombers of 154 River Road told a *Mercury* reporter just how glad he was when a helicopter began hovering over his house: "We [Sombers and his parents] were in dire need of evacuation," and "no boat could reach us in the swift-flowing current."

As night set in, the situation became extremely hazardous for the rescuers as darkness, clouds and driving rain made it very difficult to see. Pilots, with the wind pushing their copters, had to maneuver their way between tall trees, TV antennas and high-tension wires. Even for these experienced and dedicated crews, the circumstances were intimidating. One pilot stated, "I've never seen such unfavorable flying conditions in all of my career." He wryly added, "Everybody in Pottstown must have a forty-foot TV antenna." Another pilot, dumbfounded after surveying the rescue scene during daylight, frankly admitted, "If I had seen them [the obstacles] there I probably would never have tried some of the rescues I did."

Probably as harrowing as flying was making the descent to reach those stranded below. A crew member rode in a rescue net that consisted of rope netting around a steel frame that could hold two or three people. Tethered to the end of a rope, he was lowered by a hydraulic winch as the wind blew the

This aerial view shows the extent of Pottstown's flooding during Hurricane Agnes. *Courtesy of the* Pottstown Mercury.

cage around like a yo-yo at the end of its string, creating the real possibility of being smashed into a house or a tree. Corporal John Trotta made fourteen such harrowing descents. He modestly recalled that the most difficult part was talking some of the people into getting into the basket. In one instance, his powers of persuasion were futile; an "old man" told him, "You're crazy if you think I'm getting in that net." Trotta later observed with a shrug, "I guess he's still there."

The only injury was to a crew member in a basket who had one foot on a window ledge when a gust of wind buffeted the basket, causing him to lose his balance. To save himself from falling and being swept away by the raging current, he grabbed a live power line. Fortunately, he was wearing thick gloves, so his only injury was two slightly burned hands.

During the course of Thursday and Friday, four naval air rescue teams pulled 129 people, plus assorted pets, from roofs, windows and even trees.

Their efforts were undoubtedly the greatest reason nobody in the area perished during the flood.

John J. Moore, then a sergeant on the Pottstown police force, flew as a guide in one of the helicopters. In his opinion, "If the helicopters had not been available, I do not see how anyone would have been able to reach safety, and I fear that many would not have been able to survive the ordeal."

Moore was almost 100 percent correct. Happily, somebody was watching over the Kocon boys of 266 Elm Street. On Thursday night, Andy, age seven; Tony, age ten; and their big brother, "Chop," who was twelve, found themselves in the water when a boat they were riding to safety capsized. Miraculously, all of them grabbed on to a house and were able to pull themselves onto the porch roof and climb inside, where they were found safe and sound the next morning.

Perhaps the survivor with the greatest heart was Corky, a little dog that belonged to the Dickinson family, who lived at Elm and Main Street. Corky was left behind in the confusion and haste that accompanied the family's evacuation on Thursday afternoon. They feared that the dog had drowned, but when they returned on Saturday at noontime, Corky was still very much alive. She had saved herself by tenaciously clinging for two days to an automobile tire that had been left on the Dickinson's porch.

Agnes literally pummeled Pottstown. The volume of water that Schuylkill carried as it roared past and through—750,000 gallons per second—is so large that it is incomprehensible. The river's flood stage is thirteen feet; the water finally crested on Friday at thirty. At least three thousand people had been forced to evacuate one thousand homes. Those who lived in the area west of Hanover Street and south of Beech suffered the most damage, not from the river but from the Manatawny. Charles Rhoads, who had spent his entire seventy-four years in town, remarked as he shoveled mud out of his home at 170 Manatawny Street that he had witnessed "lots of floods in Pottstown" but "never saw anything like this."

Many of the industries located along the riverbank were heavily damaged; the United States Axle Company almost burned to the ground. Pottstown's water treatment plant was inundated and shut down from Thursday until Monday. During that time, residents got drinking water from tanker trucks brought in by the National Guard.

The ensuing cleanup was a long and painful process. Those who had no flood insurance suffered heavy financial losses, but the town rallied to their support. Many people did everything they could to help, from physical labor to donating food, clothing and money. A disaster relief fund raised $123,254.

Some families were so traumatized by their ordeal that they moved from the area. But the vast majority of those who had suffered stuck it out. Their fighting spirit was embodied in ninety-three-year-old Irvin Overholtzer and his seventy-three-year-old wife, Emma, who lost their home in South Pottstown and all of its contents. Undaunted, they moved into Griffith Towers at Charlotte and King Streets. In Mr. Overholtzer's words, "You're never too old to begin again."

SELECTED BIBLIOGRAPHY

Bean, Theodore W. *History of Montgomery County, Pennsylvania Illustrated.* Philadelphia, PA: 1885.

Bowman, Stanley F. *The Trolleys of Pottstown.* Thorndale, PA: self-published, 2004.

Brown, R.W. *When the Reading Came to Pottstown.* Pottstown, PA: Pottstown Historical Society, 1950.

Chancellor, Paul. *A History of Pottstown 1752–1952.* Pottstown, PA: Pottstown Historical Society, 1953.

Coco, Gregory A. *A Strange Blighted Land: Gettysburg, The Aftermath of a Battle.* Gettysburg, PA: Thomas Publications, 1995.

Davis, H.L. *The Centennial Celebration at Pottstown, PA and Historical Sketch.* Pottstown, PA: 1876.

Fisher, Joseph L.A. *The Reading's Heritage 1833–1958.* New York: Newcomen Society in North America, 1958.

Graham, Daniel. *The David Rutter (1766–1817) and Mary Ann Potts (ca. 1767–1824) Family of Pine Forge, Berks County, and Pottstown, Montgomery County, Pennsylvania.* N.p.: privately printed, 2001.

———. "General Washington's Valley Forge Land Lady, Deborah (Pyewell) Potts Hewes." *Bulletin of the Historical Society of Montgomery County Pennsylvania* 35, no. 1 (2009).

———. *Good Business Practices and Astute Matchmaking: The Ascendancy of Thomas Potts of Berks County, Pennsylvania in the Early Charcoal Iron Industry of Pennsylvania.* N.p.: privately printed, 1978.

———. "The Loyalist: John Potts, Junior." *Bulletin of the Historical Society of Montgomery County Pennsylvania* 32, no. 1 (1999).

James, Mrs. Thomas Potts. *Memorial of Thomas Potts, Junior Who Settled in Pennsylvania with a Historic-Genealogical Account of His Descendants to the Eighth Generation.* Cambridge, MA: privately printed, 1874.

Kerns, David R. *The Historic Pottstown Walking Tour.* Pottstown, PA: Pottstown 250th Anniversary Committee, 2002.

Maguire, Thomas J. *Battle of Paoli.* Mechanicsburg, PA: Stackpole Books, 2000.

Nathanson, Dr. Carol. *The Expressive Fauvism of Anne Estelle Rice.* New York: Hollis Taggart Galleries, 1997.

Pfanz, Harry W. *Gettysburg the Second Day.* Chapel Hill: University of North Carolina Press, 1987.

Ruoff, Henry Wilson. *Biographical and Portrait Cyclopedia of Montgomery County, Pennsylvania.* Philadelphia, PA: 1895.

Slovick, Kyle. "The Words and Artistry of George Yost Coffin." *GW Magazine* (Fall 2006).

Smith, Colonel Edward Martin. *The Twenty-Eighth Division Pennsylvania National Guard in the World War.* Pittsburgh, PA: The 28th Division Press, 1924.

Snyder, Michael T. "History of Pottstown: Creating a Village that Forged a Future, 1752–1802." *Pottstown Mercury*, June 2, 2002.

———. "History of Pottstown: Keeping Up With the Changing Times." *Pottstown Mercury*, August 11, 2002.

———. "History of Pottstown: A New Millennium Launches." *Pottstown Mercury*, September 8, 2002.

———. "History of Pottstown: Opening the Door to a New Century, 1802–1852." *Pottstown Mercury*, June 30, 2002.

———. "History of Pottstown: The Wounds of the War, the Healing that Followed." *Pottstown Mercury*, July 14, 2002.

———. *Saint Aloysius Roman Catholic Church, Pottstown, Pennsylvania through the Years.* Warminster, PA: Cook Publishing Company, n.d.

Stein, Irving M. *The Ginger Kid: The Buck Weaver Story.* Dubuque, IA: WCB Brown and Benchmark, 1992.

ABOUT THE AUTHOR

A retired public school teacher from Pottstown, Pennsylvania, for the last eight years Michael T. Snyder has written feature articles on local history for the *Pottstown Mercury*. He is currently the president of the Pottstown Historical Society and has lectured at many of the area's historical societies. Snyder has a keen interest in Civil War history and teaches courses on the subject at Montgomery County Community College and for the Pottstown Department of Parks and Recreation. He has also appeared as a speaker at Civil War Round Tables throughout the country, including New York City, Philadelphia, Chicago and Milwaukee.

Visit us at
www.historypress.net